The 2020 Green Bay Packers Complete Offensive Manual

Bobby Peters

ISBN: 9798559440835

DEDICATION

To Michelle and Mason.
To all those who have fostered a love of football in me.

Table of Contents

Introduction

Studying the 2020 Green Bay Packer's offense was a nice contrast from my study of the 2019 49ers. Similar base system, but two totally different approaches.

Shanahan and the 49ers were incredibly multiple with personnel and scheme choice. The Packers made a point to take the opposite approach in 2020. A clear simplification in both the run game and pass game was evident.

The offense can be described as an 11/12 personnel Zone/Duo run game with a heavy emphasis on Keepers in the play action game. With a future Hall of Fame quarterback and a true #1 wide receiver, the Packers often saw two high safeties on early downs. These two high looks from defenses allowed Green Bay to have some fantastic run looks in their lighter personnel groupings, whether running outside zone to an open bubble or getting vertical movement on inside zone and duo.

Within the simple idea of a Zone/Duo-centric system, the Packers carried plenty of adjustments and tags within those calls to have answers against different fronts and pressure looks.

The drop back pass game focuses on isolating the #1 receiver and making him the #1 read in the quarterbacks progression. Whether it is the Lookie route or isolation opposite the Middle Read – Dagger concept, Adams was the focal point of the Packers pass game. This might seem like an obvious strategy choice for Green Bay, but many

NFL teams fail to do this for true top-tier wide receivers. What made this work for Green Bay was that Adams most often won his 1 on 1 matchups with excellent releases at the line of scrimmage, separation at the top of the route, and winning contested catches with well-thrown balls from Rodgers.

Front Glossary

The following bullet points describe the fronts used in the statistical break downs in this book.

- Bear: Head up nose with two 3 techniques. Part of the odd front family.

- Over: 4 down with a 3 technique and a 1/2i nose guard.

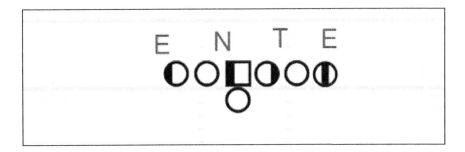

- Under: Even front with the nose shaded strong. Often times the defense will walk the Sam up on the end of the line of scrimmage in this front as well.

- Wide: Even Front with two 3 techniques

- Odd: 4-0-4. Head up ends on the tackles with a head up nose.

- 6-Man: An even front with the Sam and Will walked up on the line of scrimmage. The interior can be some combination of one gap and two gap principles. This defensive front became popularized against the Shanahan/McVay/LaFleur type offense when the Patriots used it to stifle the Rams in the Super Bowl of the 2018 season.

- Diamond: Similar structure to a bear front, but linebackers walked up into the interior gaps instead of down lineman. This is a common front in passing situations.

- Mug: An even front with the interior linebackers walked up into their gaps. This is another common front in passing situations.

Coverage Glossary

The following bullet points serve as definitions for all of the coverages referenced in this book. The coverage data should be taken with a grain of salt, as coverages are often hard to determine without knowing the call. For instance, the four vertical concept would play out similarly for a cover 3 zone match coverage as it would for cover 1.

- Cover 0: Man coverage with no safety help. There could still be a rat/hole player with these calls.
- Cover 1: Single high man coverage with a low hole/rat. Some calls have the rat/hole player double a specific receiver.
- Cover 2: spot drop zone and zone match cover 2 (Includes Tampa 2)
- Cover 3: Single high zone/zone match coverage
- Cover 4: Quarters (mainly zone match)
- Cover 5: Man under two deep. This section does include some of the Saban cover 7 (man match quarters) calls that play out like man under two deep.
- Cover 42: Quarters to one side, cover 2 to the other.
- Drop 8: Eight dropped into coverage (3 man rush)
- 5 Man Pressure: Any call that involves five rushers. The coverage call could be any of the above-listed coverages.

General Notes

- The label "TO" in the charts stands for Turnover.
- The blank down and distance plays are two point conversion attempts.
- The numbers in parenthesis next to each title denotes the personnel grouping. The number of running backs listed as the first digit, the number of tight ends listed as the second digit.
- PSG = Play Side Guard
- PST = Play Side Tackle
- BSG = Back Side Guard
- BST = Back Side Tackle
- PSWR = Play Side Wide Receiver

Outside Zone Weak (12/11/10/20)

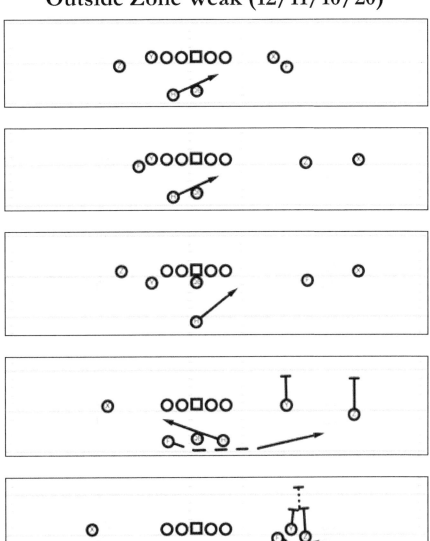

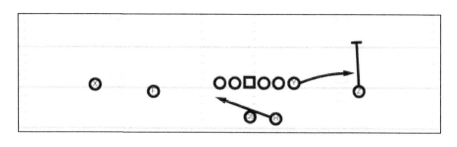

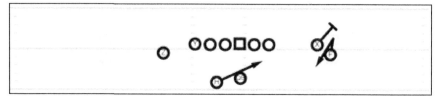

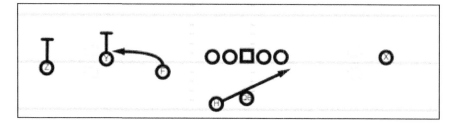

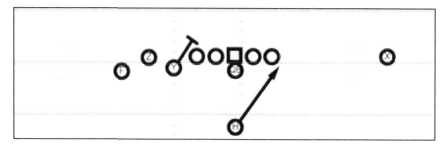

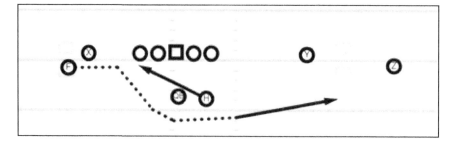

Average Yards per Play	5.3

1st Down		3rd/4th Down (includes RZ)	
Called	Average	Called	Success Rate
23	5.1	0	0%
2nd Down 6-1		2nd Down 7+	
Called	Average	Called	Average
11	6.3	13	4.7
Red Zone 10-0		Red Zone 10-20	
Called	Touchdown %	Called	Touchdown %
4	0%	1	0%

Bear		Over		6-Man	
Called	Average	Called	Average	Called	Average
1	8.0	26	5.2	0	0.0
Under (4 Man)		Mug		Under Sam Up	
Called	Average	Called	Average	Called	Average
12	5.0	1	9.0	2	3.0
Wide		Odd		Diamond	
Called	Average	Called	Average	Called	Average
1	4.0	2	9.5	0	0.0

Week	Quarter	Time	Down	ToGo	Location	Yards
Week 1 vs MN	2	11:20	1	10	GNB 49	5
Week 1 vs MN	2	6:04	1	10	GNB 40	6
Week 1 vs MN	3	8:20	2	7	GNB 40	1
Week 1 vs MN	3	4:13	2	10	GNB 39	3
Week 1 vs MN	4	6:26	1	10	GNB 37	4
Week 2 vs DET	1	0:04	1	10	GNB 25	4
Week 2 vs DET	2	10:53	2	5	DET 9	2
Week 2 vs DET	3	11:14	1	10	DET 36	4
Week 2 vs DET	4	6:14	1	10	GNB 36	3
Week 3 vs NO	4	5:17	1	10	NOR 22	5
Week 4 vs ATL	1	12:50	1	10	ATL 46	8
Week 4 vs ATL	1	6:51	2	2	ATL 20	-5
Week 4 vs ATL	1	5:34	1	6	ATL 6	3
Week 4 vs ATL	3	13:26	1	10	GNB 33	-3
Week 6 vs TB	2	0:37	3	1	GNB 34	5
Week 8 vs MIN	1	13:00	2	4	GNB 43	10
Week 8 vs MIN	1	10:35	2	6	MIN 29	4
Week 8 vs MIN	3	4:26	1	10	GNB 49	1
Week 9 vs SF	3	4:46	1	10	SFO 23	9
Week 9 vs SF	4	13:46	2	7	GNB 8	3
Week 10 vs JAX	1	1:04	2	10	GNB 9	7
Week 10 vs JAX	2	5:55	2	7	JAX 37	6
Week 10 vs JAX	2	3:06	1	8	JAX 8	3
Week 10 vs JAX	3	9:51	2	6	GNB 29	14
Week 10 vs JAX	3	8:09	2	5	JAX 35	2
Week 11 vs IND	2	10:38	1	5	CLT 25	23
Week 11 vs IND	4	7:23	1	10	GNB 33	0
Week 11 vs IND	OT	9:20	2	2	GNB 30	-1
Week 13 vs PHI	2	12:28	2	1	PHI 27	3
Week 13 vs PHI	2	11:43	1	10	PHI 24	6
Week 13 vs PHI	2	4:43	1	10	GNB 18	1
Week 14 vs DET	1	2:56	2	7	DET 45	6
Week 14 vs DET	3	12:11	1	10	DET 49	11
Week 15 vs CAR	1	13:33	2	10	GNB 19	9
Week 15 vs CAR	1	11:25	1	10	CAR 14	6
Week 15 vs CAR	1	0:26	2	2	CAR 24	14
Week 15 vs CAR	2	6:03	1	10	CAR 24	3
Week 15 vs CAR	2	2:47	1	10	GNB 37	4
Week 15 vs CAR	2	0:26	2	16	GNB 25	3
Week 15 vs CAR	3	4:04	2	8	GNB 42	4
Week 16 vs TEN	1	0:31	2	10	OTI 30	9
Week 16 vs TEN	2	7:31	2	8	OTI 30	5
Week 17 vs CHI	2	7:11	1	11	CHI 23	3
Week 17 vs CHI	4	8:15	1	10	GNB 49	8
Week 17 vs CHI	4	6:11	2	6	CHI 36	17
DIV vs LAR	1	12:13	1	10	GNB 42	9
DIV vs LAR	1	11:35	2	1	RAM 49	3
DIV vs LAR	1	10:10	2	10	RAM 34	3
DIV vs LAR	3	8:29	2	10	GNB 40	2
NFCCG vs TB	2	9:40	2	5	TAM 42	12
NFCCG vs TB	2	8:12	2	1	TAM 21	3
NFCCG vs TB	4	2:22	1	8	TAM 8	0

The general idea of running outside zone weak is to run to the open B-gap bubble. In an Over front, which is the front most commonly run against 11 personnel formations, the B gap bubble is weak. The center will reach the nose and the play side guard will work up to the Will. The next diagram shows the most common look.

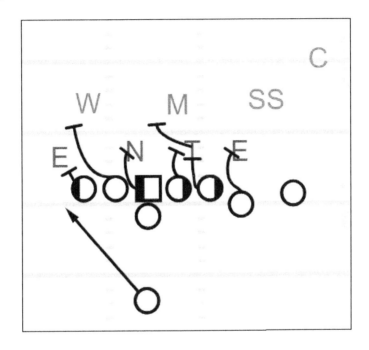

The PST's block is important for keeping that B-gap bubble open. If the PST does not get any movement, the reach block of the center can end up hip to hip with the PST and close the B-gap. A good landmark to watch for is if the PST can base the end out to the numbers. If the two of them end up on the numbers, the B-gap should have a chance.

Some defenses will have their nose play a 2i instead of a 1 technique. This changes the frontside combination most of the time. With a 2i, the center will have the help of the PSG. This is drawn up in the next section. Against this look, the play will more likely cut off the 3 technique. The ability of the BST to cut off/reach the 3 technique is critical. Against fast flowing linebackers, the offense might be better off checking to a strong side outside zone run vs a 2i.

RPO's are commonly used with Outside Zone Weak in the Packers' offense. Bubbles/Nows/Arrows were the most common. With he use of quick motions and bunch formations, Rodgers was able to take advantage of 3 over 2 or 2 over 1 situations on the edge and get the ball out with his lightning-quick release.

Why it Worked: In week 9, Rodgers gets the ball to Adams on the bunch bubble screen against a two high look. Tonyan and MVS do a nice job of double teaming the point up to the corner.

In week 8, the Packers get a light box with a backfield motion-bubble RPO removing the Mike. The PST gets the DE to the numbers, the C and PSG combo the nose up to the Will. Adams push cracks the free safety (Harrison Smith) forcing the corner to make the tackle 10 yards downfield.

The five yard gain in week 1 shows how the play can still work if the offensive line can not reach the down front. With the front working horizontally not to get reached, the offensive line gets vertical movement. Ervin presses his read, then cuts behind the vertical movement of the BST.

Week 3 4Q shows a nice clip of the BST reaching the 3

technique against an Over (2i). Great help from the BSG as well.

Why it Didn't Work: Week 13 2Q 4:43 the Packers run it to the 3 technique. The PSG is able to reach the 3 tech, but he is able to fight over the top once the running back makes his cut.

Outside Zone Weak – Fake Jet (12/11/10)

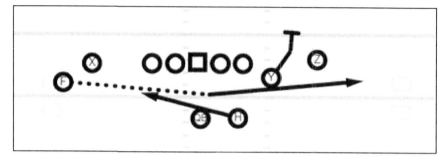

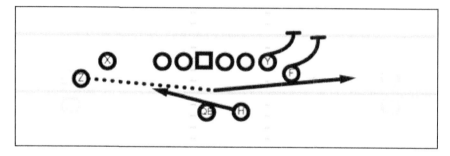

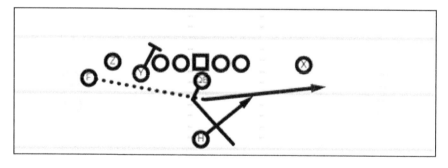

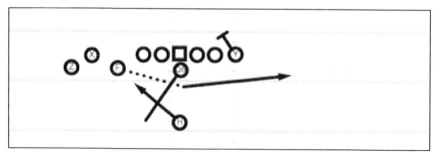

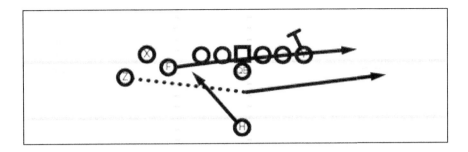

Average Yards per Play	4.2

1st Down		3rd/4th Down (includes RZ)	
Called	Average	Called	Success Rate
18	3.7	1	100%
2nd Down 6-1		**2nd Down 7+**	
Called	Average	Called	Average
7	6.4	3	1.7
Red Zone 10-0		**Red Zone 10-20**	
Called	Touchdown %	Called	Touchdown %
0	0%	0	0%

Bear		Over		6-Man	
Called	Average	Called	Average	Called	Average
1	3.0	21	4.4	0	0.0
Under (4 Man)		**Mug**		**Under Sam Up**	
Called	Average	Called	Average	Called	Average
4	2.5	0	0.0	1	12.0
Wide		**Odd**		**Diamond**	
Called	Average	Called	Average	Called	Average
0	0.0	1	2.0	0	0.0

Week	Quarter	Time	Down	ToGo	Location	Yards
Week 1 vs MN	1	10:24	2	1	MIN 27	2
Week 1 vs MN	3	9:06	1	10	GNB 37	3
Week 1 vs MN	4	7:55	1	10	GNB 25	5
Week 3 vs NO	1	11:51	1	10	GNB 44	2
Week 3 vs NO	4	10:16	1	10	NOR 35	3
Week 4 vs ATL	1	12:08	2	2	ATL 38	9
Week 4 vs ATL	2	6:59	1	10	GNB 42	3
Week 4 vs ATL	3	12:43	2	13	GNB 30	0
Week 4 vs ATL	4	8:55	1	10	ATL 40	12
Week 6 vs TB	1	8:20	1	10	GNB 20	5
Week 7 vs HOU	1	14:22	2	7	GNB 28	5
Week 7 vs HOU	2	2:03	2	10	GNB 46	0
Week 8 vs MIN	1	13:41	1	10	GNB 37	6
Week 8 vs MIN	2	13:33	1	20	GNB 30	8
Week 8 vs MIN	2	12:19	1	10	MIN 46	1
Week 8 vs MIN	2	9:40	3	2	MIN 23	6
Week 8 vs MIN	3	10:00	1	10	GNB 25	3
Week 9 vs SF	1	0:47	1	10	GNB 25	2
Week 10 vs JAX	2	10:01	1	10	GNB 19	4
Week 11 vs IND	1	12:27	1	10	GNB 49	7
Week 11 vs IND	1	9:06	1	10	CLT 26	1
Week 11 vs IND	3	7:39	1	10	GNB 14	3
Week 15 vs CAR	1	5:57	1	10	GNB 25	2
Week 15 vs CAR	1	2:27	2	4	CAR 49	3
Week 16 vs TEN	1	12:58	2	2	OTI 42	12
Week 16 vs TEN	3	7:02	1	5	OTI 44	-3
Week 16 vs TEN	4	7:41	2	4	GNB 15	8
Week 17 vs CHI	1	5:26	2	1	GNB 43	10
Week 17 vs CHI	1	1:55	2	6	CHI 26	1
NFCCG vs TB	4	2:15	3	8	TAM 8	0

This concept is a good way to get a hat for a hat on the outside zone scheme. With the fake jet motion and the TE arcing, the defensive end will often widen just enough to create the backside C-gap cutback lane. The image below shows this playing out. This often was the case against Minnesota. Zimmer and the Vikings like to play their strong end in a head up six technique in their base over front. If the defensive end is influenced by the motion and TE arc, the cutback lane is there.

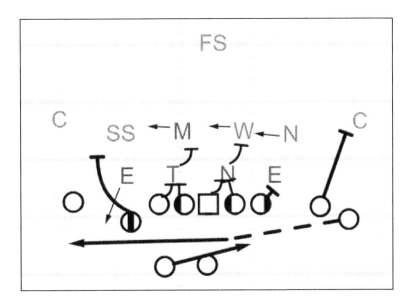

Many NFL defenses will play their base over front with a 1 technique instead of a 2i. With a 1 technique, the Packers would often leave the center on him 1 on 1 and have the PSG hep the PST with the end before climbing to the second level. The next image shows the difference with a 1 tech instead of a 2i.

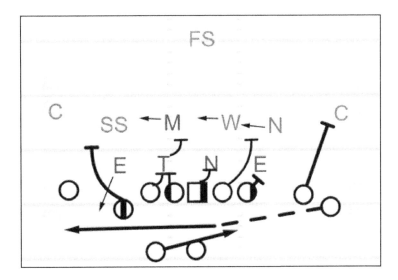

With the fast jet motion, defenses are often forced to get their nickel into the front side A-gap run fit. The mike linebacker will typically have to bump out of the fit as a result. This takes out a primary run defender and puts a primary pass defender in the box.

Against base odd front defenses, the Packers won't arc the tight end as much. Against 11 personnel, the odd front defenses will typically sub out and end and play an even front. The matchup for the TE to block a stand up OLB playing DE is safe enough for the offense.

On a couple occasions, the Packers would run the fake jet to the same side as the zone run (shown in the 3rd diagram). This serves to soften/widen the play side defensive end

Why it Worked: In the first clip of week 16, the Packers get the backers to bump hard with he jet motion, making the center's combo up to the first linebacker much easier. Adams digs out the cover 4 safety at the point of attack as well.

The Packers pick up a 3rd & 2 in week 8 hitting the cutback lane with the widened defensive end.

The last clip in week 16 shows the nub-bunch variation shown in the 4th diagram. In Tennessee's single high structure, they burn three players, the strong safety, corner, and defensive end on the weak side of the play.

Why it Didn't Work: In week 11, the play side 3 tech gets penetration in a 1 on 1 situation and forces an early cutback.

Outside Zone Slice (11/20)

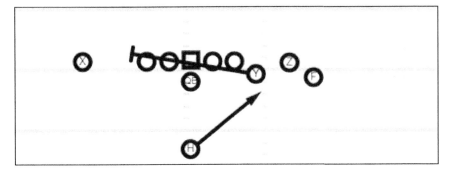

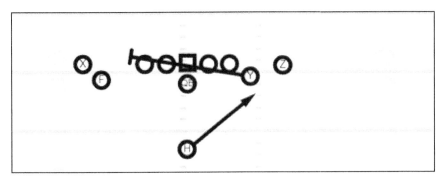

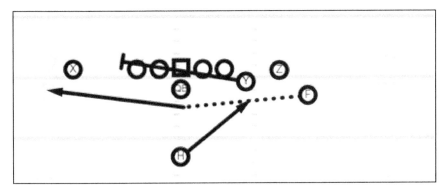

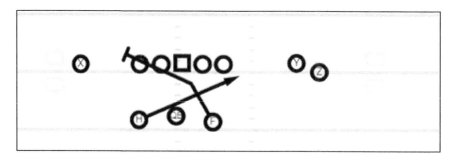

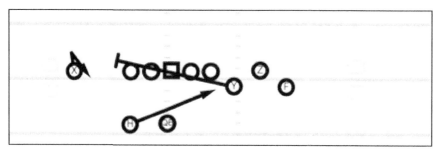

Average Yards per Play	3.7

1st Down		3rd/4th Down (includes RZ)	
Called	Average	Called	Success Rate
15	4.0	1	0%
2nd Down 6-1		**2nd Down 7+**	
Called	Average	Called	Average
3	4.7	3	2.3
Red Zone 10-0		**Red Zone 10-20**	
Called	Touchdown %	Called	Touchdown %
2	0%	2	0%

Bear		Over		6-Man	
Called	Average	Called	Average	Called	Average
5	1.6	10	2.4	1	9.0
Under (4 Man)		**Mug**		**Under Sam Up**	
Called	Average	Called	Average	Called	Average
3	8.0	1	0.0	0	0.0
Wide		**Odd**		**Diamond**	
Called	Average	Called	Average	Called	Average
0	0.0	0	0.0	1	7.0

Week	Quarter	Time	Down	ToGo	Location	Yards
Week 1 vs MN	1	14:16	2	8	GNB 27	4
Week 1 vs MN	1	11:33	2	3	MIN 45	9
Week 1 vs MN	3	9:50	1	10	GNB 22	15
Week 2 vs DET	1	6:34	1	10	DET 32	7
Week 3 vs NO	1	11:19	2	8	GNB 46	1
Week 3 vs NO	2	11:20	1	2	NOR 2	-3
Week 3 vs NO	2	3:36	2	10	GNB 35	2
Week 4 vs ATL	1	7:34	1	10	ATL 28	8
Week 4 vs ATL	4	3:33	2	6	GNB 30	5
Week 7 vs HOU	3	4:55	2	4	HTX 45	0
Week 8 vs MIN	1	12:22	1	10	MIN 47	9
Week 8 vs MIN	4	11:06	1	10	GNB 36	9
Week 9 vs SF	1	10:08	1	10	GNB 20	2
Week 10 vs JAX	1	9:33	1	10	JAX 45	1
Week 12 vs CHI	1	8:18	1	10	CHI 12	0
Week 12 vs CHI	2	6:04	1	10	CHI 14	5
Week 12 vs CHI	4	8:51	3	13	GNB 40	0
Week 12 vs CHI	4	3:20	1	10	CHI 47	0
Week 13 vs PHI	1	1:11	1	10	GNB 12	1
Week 16 vs TEN	1	5:50	1	10	GNB 20	1
Week 16 vs TEN	1	2:30	1	10	GNB 40	6
Week 16 vs TEN	3	11:17	1	7	OTI 7	-1

Split-flow outside zone is a complimentary play for outside zone heavy teams. Split flow on outside zone can often mess with linebackers more than it would with inside zone, as the horizontal displacement is greater. For defenses that like to "fall back" their run fits, the linebackers have a lot of ground to cover and choose the right gap in a short amount of time.

The read for the running back remains the same. He will aim for the original alignment of the tight end and read the play outside-in.

Against single high coverages, the Packers will often use the play side condensed receivers to dig out any rolled down safety or secondary player.

Against fast flowing linebackers on a two high defense, the cutback lane could be huge. If the backside linebacker pursues the zone action, the back side C gap might not have a defender present.

The drive block for the play side tackle is easier with split flow action as well. With the tight end originally lined up on the play side, the defensive end will be wider and will often have eyes on the tight end at some point during the play.

Why it Worked: Week 1 3Q shows how the split flow outside zone can cause confusion at the second level. The Mike does not fall back with the split flow, while the Will does. This leaves a huge hole in the back side A-gap. The PSG gets up on the Mike quickly as well, which does not allow him to react to the cutback from Jones. The next image shows the action.

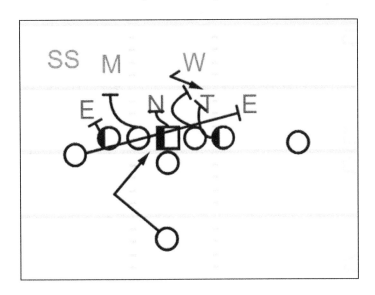

Why it Didn't Work: In week 16, the Packers push the blocks back and leave the play side CB unblocked. The CB forces the ball back into the play side defensive end.

In general, there seemed to be some confusion on this concept for the Packers. On a few occasions, the offensive line and play side wide receiver would work to the same defender, leaving an inside linebacker free.

Outside Zone Strong – 1 TE (11/12)

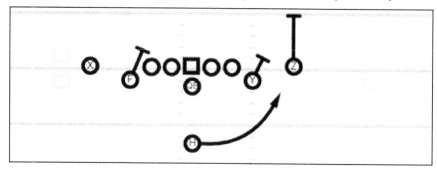

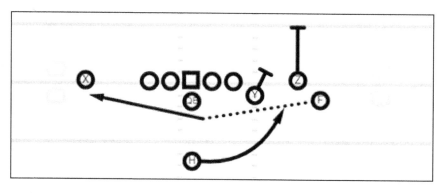

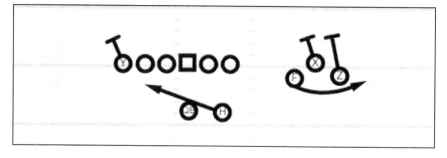

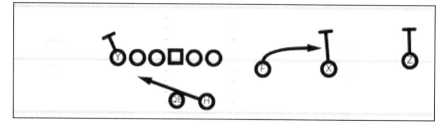

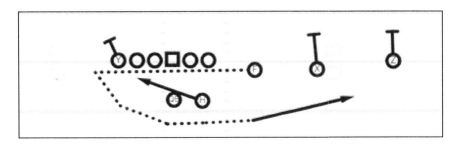

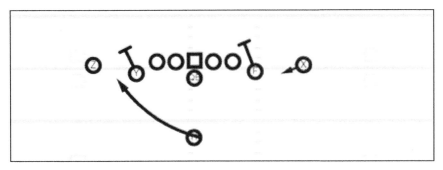

Average Yards per Play	4.1

1st Down		3rd/4th Down (includes RZ)	
Called	Average	Called	Success Rate
17	4.6	4	50%
2nd Down 6-1		**2nd Down 7+**	
Called	Average	Called	Average
4	5.5	3	4.0
Red Zone 10-0		**Red Zone 10-20**	
Called	Touchdown %	Called	Touchdown %
2	0%	4	25%

Bear		Over		6-Man	
Called	Average	Called	Average	Called	Average
1	8.0	20	4.0	0	0.0
Under (4 Man)		Mug		Under Sam Up	
Called	Average	Called	Average	Called	Average
1	4.0	1	5.0	3	0.3
Wide		Odd		Diamond	
Called	Average	Called	Average	Called	Average
0	0.0	3	7.0	0	0.0

Week	Quarter	Time	Down	ToGo	Location	Yards
Week 2 vs DET	4	8:05	1	10	DET 14	14
Week 3 vs NO	1	10:21	3	2	NOR 48	5
Week 3 vs NO	1	0:33	1	10	NOR 20	3
Week 3 vs NO	3	3:51	1	10	NOR 26	5
Week 4 vs ATL	2	6:18	2	7	GNB 45	8
Week 6 vs TB	1	15:00	1	10	GNB 25	0
Week 6 vs TB	1	14:18	2	10	GNB 25	0
Week 6 vs TB	3	6:31	1	10	GNB 45	0
Week 6 vs TB	4	10:14	2	10	GNB 41	4
Week 9 vs SF	3	4:13	2	1	SFO 14	4
Week 9 vs SF	4	7:03	3	15	SFO 35	0
Week 10 vs JAX	2	11:04	3	2	GNB 35	-3
Week 10 vs JAX	3	2:06	1	10	JAX 49	0
Week 10 vs JAX	4	12:40	1	10	GNB 25	1
Week 13 vs PHI	2	1:51	2	5	PHI 26	1
Week 13 vs PHI	4	6:22	1	10	GNB 22	1
Week 14 vs DET	3	4:10	1	10	GNB 36	8
Week 14 vs DET	3	3:26	2	2	GNB 44	-1
Week 14 vs DET	4	12:47	3	1	DET 8	4
Week 14 vs DET	4	5:08	1	10	GNB 36	29
Week 14 vs DET	4	4:33	1	10	DET 35	1
Week 14 vs DET	4	1:49	1	10	DET 45	4
Week 15 vs CAR	2	2:09	2	6	GNB 41	18
Week 15 vs CAR	3	4:41	1	10	GNB 40	2
Week 15 vs CAR	4	5:15	1	10	CAR 29	2
Week 16 vs TEN	1	4:26	1	10	GNB 35	1
Week 16 vs TEN	2	14:54			OTI 2	0
Week 16 vs TEN	2	12:39	1	10	OTI 20	6

The differentiating factor for this version of outside zone strong is the play side corner is accounted for and blocked. In most cases it's the PSWR blocking him, but in a nub formation the tight end and PST are combo'ing the defensive end to the corner.

Running this concept against an Over front can be challenging if the defense plays the nose shading the center. The BSG must scoop hard to reach with he help of the center. If this reach block is not made, the running back will have to cut back into an often unblocked defensive end. Against these looks, outside zone weak is the preferred play call.

This play becomes more of a useful concept if the defense plays the nose in a 2i on the guard. This was the case against New Orleans, Philadelphia, and the second matchup with Detroit.

The Packers will often use their slot receiver in 11 personnel to seal off the back side defensive end. Instead of the back side defensive end being the unblocked player, now the nickel will be unblocked. This exchange is a win for the offense as the nickel is not as big of a danger to stopping the play. The next diagram shows the action with a short motion from the slot. The Packers also run it with him lined up there initially.

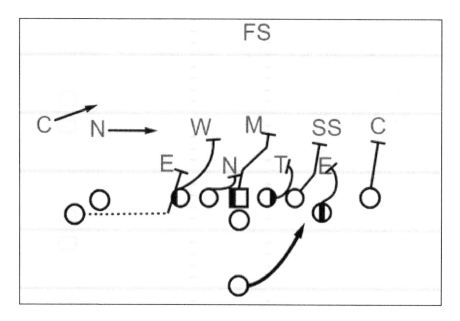

The Nub – Bubble RPO was the most common RPO version called in 2020. Rodgers liked to throw the bubble against heavy fronts and against pressure looks. The Packers' receivers often double teamed the most dangerous defender and worked to the next most dangerous. In general, the Packers block bubble screens well.

Why it Worked: In week 14, Rodgers hits Adams on the back side Now route shown in the sixth diagram. The Lions play cover 3 and have the corner aligned off.

Why it Didn't Work: On 3rd and 2 in week 10, Rodgers throws the bubble with 3 over 3 in a version of man coverage. The unblocked DB makes the tackle behind the line of scrimmage.

Outside Zone Strong – 2 TE (12)

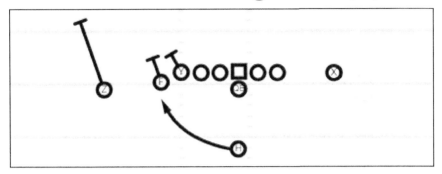

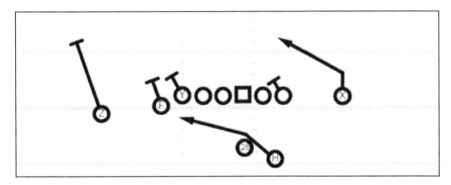

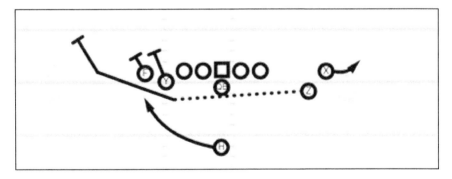

Average Yards per Play	5.3

1st Down		3rd/4th Down (includes RZ)	
Called	Average	Called	Success Rate
5	8.2	0	0%
2nd Down 6-1		**2nd Down 7+**	
Called	Average	Called	Average
2	0.5	1	0.0
Red Zone 10-0		**Red Zone 10-20**	
Called	Touchdown %	Called	Touchdown %
0	0%	0	0%

Bear		Over		6-Man	
Called	Average	Called	Average	Called	Average
3	8.0	1	0.0	1	3.0
Under (4 Man)		**Mug**		**Under Sam Up**	
Called	Average	Called	Average	Called	Average
0	0.0	0	0.0	2	0.0
Wide		**Odd**		**Diamond**	
Called	Average	Called	Average	Called	Average
0	0.0	1	15.0	0	0.0

Week	Quarter	Time	Down	ToGo	Location	Yards
Week 1 vs MN	4	12:29	1	10	MIN 46	3
Week 2 vs DET	3	7:33	1	10	GNB 14	11
Week 6 vs TB	1	4:28	1	10	TAM 26	13
Week 6 vs TB	2	12:04	2	3	GNB 32	0
Week 9 vs SF	3	12:32	2	7	GNB 23	0
Week 12 vs CHI	1	2:35	2	5	CHI 29	1
Week 12 vs CHI	2	9:29	1	10	GNB 49	15
Week 17 vs CHI	1	4:46	1	10	CHI 47	-1

Similar to the 2 TE inside zone and duo concepts, this play is a great way to get a double team on the defensive end/Sam. This is especially the case against odd fronts with the PST occupied by a head up 4 technique. The next diagram shows this against a Bear front. With the defense in a cover 2 shell, the back side of the offensive line will base back to the stand up outside linebacker outside of the BST. The PST will help on the play side 3 technique as well, creating two double teams at the point of attack.

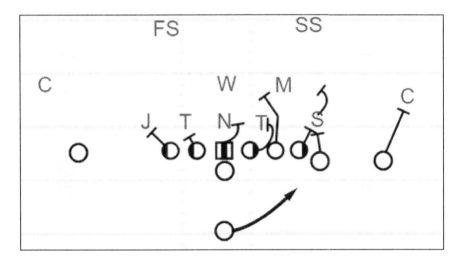

Against a single high defense, the double teams will have to push to a play side linebacker. This scheme accounts for all of the box defenders in a single high structure with the PSWR blocking the corner. The next diagram shows this drawn up.

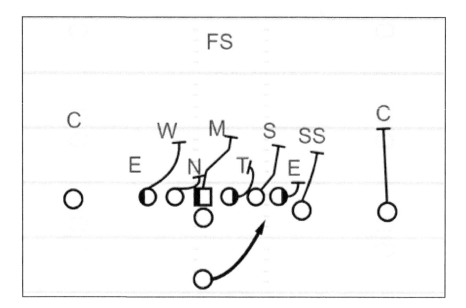

The 2nd diagram shows a common RPO used with this concept in many Shanahan systems. Against loaded fronts with no 2nd level support in the weak hook at the snap, the quick slant is an alert for the quarterback.

Why it Worked: The Packers hit a couple of their RPO's for big plays in 2020 off this run. In week 6, the Bucs play with a bear front, leaving no off-ball help for the back side slant window.

In week 12, Rodgers pops the now screen to Adams in space vs an off cover 3 corner for a big play. The now screen is particularly useful when paired with the escort motion and the safety/nickel bumps hard inside to take a run gap. If the QB gets the ball out quick, the adjusting corner is left in a 1 on 1 from depth.

In week 2, the Packers are able to double team the Sam vs a Bear front and get the ball to the edge.

Why it Didn't Work: In week 6, the Bucs use a Bear front to keep their middle linebacker free to chase down the play. The center is not able to get to the fast flow middle linebacker in space. The play side 3 technique slanting inside also knocks the center off his path. Great scheme to slow down outside zone from Todd Bowles and the Bucs defense.

Outside Zone Strong "Back" (11/12/13)

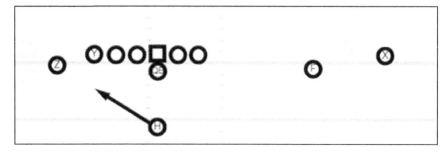

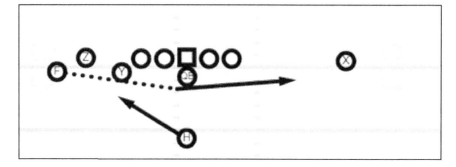

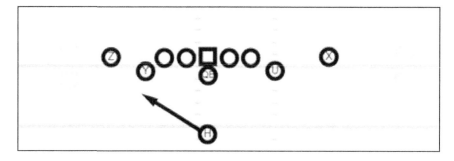

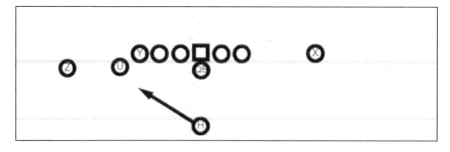

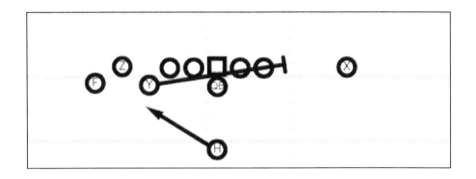

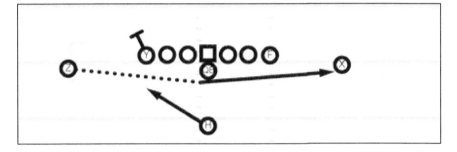

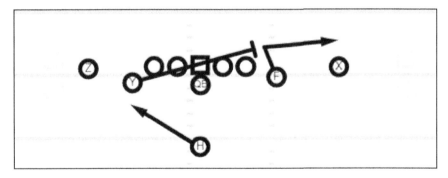

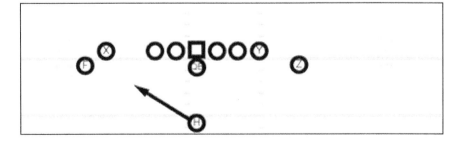

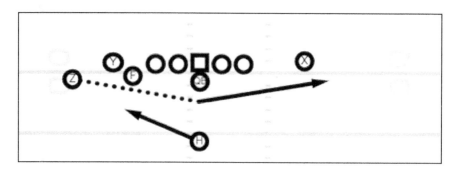

Average Yards per Play	5.4

1st Down		3rd/4th Down (includes RZ)	
Called	Average	Called	Success Rate
18	6.0	0	0%
2nd Down 6-1		**2nd Down 7+**	
Called	Average	Called	Average
9	4.2	5	2.8
Red Zone 10-0		**Red Zone 10-20**	
Called	Touchdown %	Called	Touchdown %
0	0%	3	0%

Bear		Over		6-Man	
Called	Average	Called	Average	Called	Average
5	4.6	17	4.9	0	0.0
Under (4 Man)		**Mug**		**Under Sam Up**	
Called	Average	Called	Average	Called	Average
4	4.3	0	0.0	3	6.0
Wide		**Odd**		**Diamond**	
Called	Average	Called	Average	Called	Average
0	0.0	3	10.0	0	0.0

Week	Quarter	Time	Down	ToGo	Location	Yards
Week 1 vs MN	1	14:16	2	8	GNB 27	4
Week 2 vs DET	4	2:13	1	10	DET 40	-1
Week 4 vs ATL	3	6:39	1	10	ATL 28	6
Week 4 vs ATL	4	12:52	1	10	GNB 25	11
Week 6 vs TB	1	11:24	2	10	TAM 23	2
Week 8 vs MIN	2	15:00	2	3	GNB 35	2
Week 9 vs SF	1	14:30	2	5	GNB 30	11
Week 9 vs SF	2	11:00	1	10	SFO 27	6
Week 9 vs SF	4	12:24	1	10	GNB 45	8
Week 10 vs JAX	1	8:50	2	9	JAX 44	7
Week 10 vs JAX	1	1:47	1	10	GNB 9	0
Week 10 vs JAX	4	4:06	1	10	GNB 14	5
Week 10 vs JAX	4	3:23	2	5	GNB 19	4
Week 11 vs IND	1	5:35	2	10	GNB 34	1
Week 12 vs CHI	1	13:32	1	10	GNB 50	1
Week 12 vs CHI	1	9:40	2	2	CHI 17	1
Week 13 vs PHI	4	15:00	2	3	PHI 40	3
Week 14 vs DET	3	1:57	1	10	DET 46	9
Week 15 vs CAR	1	12:08	1	10	CAR 26	12
Week 15 vs CAR	2	6:59	1	10	CAR 37	6
Week 15 vs CAR	2	6:33	2	4	CAR 31	7
Week 15 vs CAR	2	6:03	1	10	CAR 24	3
Week 15 vs CAR	3	5:15	1	10	GNB 25	10
Week 16 vs TEN	1	11:30	1	10	OTI 17	5
Week 16 vs TEN	2	5:22	2	5	OTI 14	-3
Week 16 vs TEN	3	8:43	1	10	GNB 37	8
Week 16 vs TEN	3	5:45	1	10	OTI 39	8
Week 16 vs TEN	4	14:48	1	10	GNB 43	10
Week 16 vs TEN	4	4:48	2	10	OTI 41	0
DIV vs LAR	1	0:38	2	4	RAM 47	8
NFCCG vs TB	2	10:59	2	6	GNB 41	12
NFCCG vs TB	3	13:54	1	10	GNB 25	6

Outside Zone "Back" is a nice way to force the ball to the edge on outside zone. I use the term "Back" to describe the offensive line working one linebacker back.

Often times against single high defenses, the offensive line has to work hard to get to their play side linebacker in regular outside zone schemes. This "Back" adjustment makes running outside zone easier against these looks.

The "Back" call allows for longer double teams and will help prevent linebackers from scraping over the top. The action often looks like a swinging gate, with he back side tackle being the hinge. The diagram below shows the play out of a balanced 12 personnel formation. The Z receiver is the adjuster here to block the strong safety.

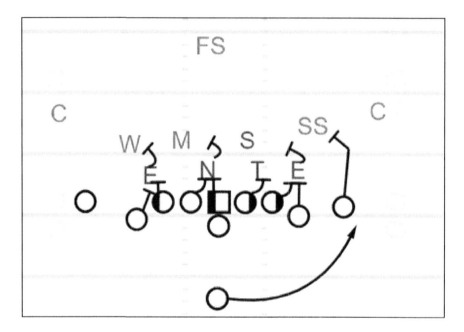

The one drawback is the play side corner will often be unblocked. If the other team has a corner that is not a good tackler, then this version becomes even more appealing.

Against cover 2/4, the PSWR will block the most dangerous man between the corner and near safety.

The offense can gain an extra play side blocker when called out of 12 or 21 personnel with a 2 TE or TE/FB surface . The added benefit with this version is the ability to double team the 3 technique with the PST. The two tight ends can work the DE in tandem to the force/strong safety in a 3x1 set or the off ball Sam in a 2x2 Slot formation. The diagram below shows how the PSG can get some help with this version.

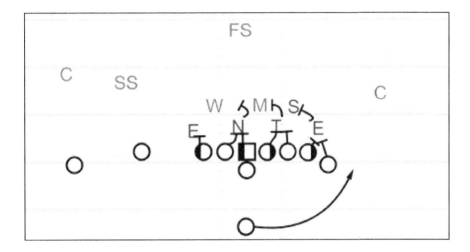

The Packers will also call fake jet motion with this version to create misdirection and swap out a linebacker for a safety in the run fit.

Most of the Outside Zone teams (Shanahan, McVay) will exclusively run their "back" concepts to the tight end. I believe Lafleur started calling them weak (and with a slice) in 2020. It is hard to tell on film if these are calls, or the O-Line or PSWR's mess up. Most of these look sloppy, as the O-line is working to the same player as a PSWR. On these versions, the ability for a WR to get horizontal and dig out a box nickel/linebacker becomes critical. Also, the PST will try harder to reach the defensive end as the play wants to hit outside.

Why it Worked: Creating easier angles and allowing for longer double teams allows the offense to take care of the most dangerous defenders and get the RB out in space. Especially if corners don't want to come up and tackle, this can be a deadly version of outside zone.

This concept is very useful against fast flow linebackers that can easily avoid a play side reach. With the O-Line working back a linebacker, the fast flow can be negated easier. This concept worked well against Tampa Bay's defense in the NFC Championship Game.

In week 14, the Packers run the 2 TE Slot version against an over front. the 3 technique ends up making the tackle 8 yards downfield, but with better help from the PST, the 3 tech could have been reached.

In week 4, the Packers bring an extra tackle in at tight end for some extra cheese. The Falcons roll to cover two late, which creates even better angles for the offensive line.

Why it Didn't Work: Aggressive corners are often the biggest hindrance to this concept. In week 13, the corner gets physical and makes a nice tackle for a short gain.

Outside Zone Strong - Lead (21/11/22)

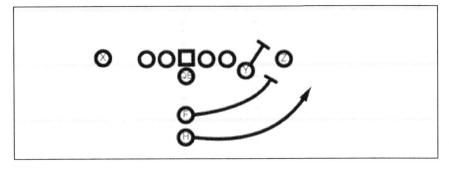

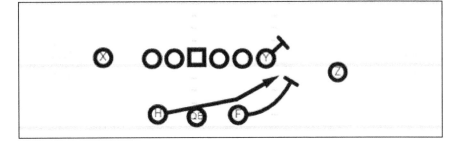

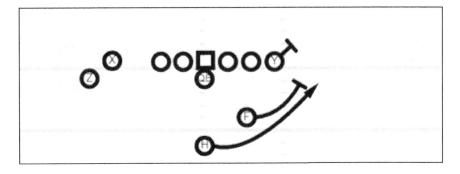

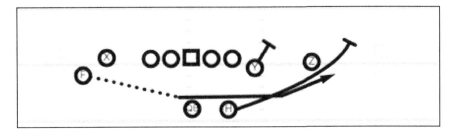

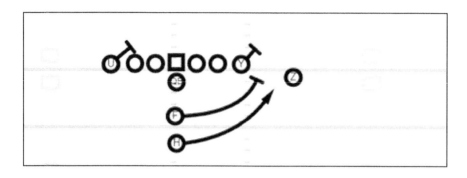

Average Yards per Play	3.8

1st Down		3rd/4th Down (includes RZ)	
Called	Average	Called	Success Rate
11	3.3	1	100%
2nd Down 6-1		**2nd Down 7+**	
Called	Average	Called	Average
3	4.7	2	1.0
Red Zone 10-0		**Red Zone 10-20**	
Called	Touchdown %	Called	Touchdown %
3	33%	1	0%

Bear		Over		6-Man	
Called	Average	Called	Average	Called	Average
5	5.2	9	1.9	1	4.0
Under (4 Man)		**Mug**		**Under Sam Up**	
Called	Average	Called	Average	Called	Average
0	0.0	0	0.0	2	8.5
Wide		**Odd**		**Diamond**	
Called	Average	Called	Average	Called	Average
0	0.0	0	0.0	0	0.0

Week	Quarter	Time	Down	ToGo	Location	Yards
Week 1 vs MN	1	15:00	1	10	GNB 25	2
Week 1 vs MN	1	8:50	1	10	MIN 10	-1
Week 1 vs MN	2	9:59	1	10	MIN 28	4
Week 1 vs MN	2	2:13	1	10	MIN 37	4
Week 2 vs DET	2	5:31	2	2	GNB 18	11
Week 2 vs DET	4	1:54	3	11	DET 41	12
Week 4 vs ATL	4	3:16	1	10	ATL 45	-1
Week 6 vs TB	1	3:09	1	20	TAM 23	0
Week 6 vs TB	3	12:14	1	10	GNB 25	4
Week 6 vs TB	4	7:05	1	10	GNB 30	3
Week 6 vs TB	4	6:31	2	7	GNB 33	1
Week 7 vs HOU	1	10:11	2	3	HTX 3	0
Week 7 vs HOU	4	4:30	1	10	HTX 14	13
Week 8 vs MIN	4	9:06	2	10	MIN 33	1
Week 13 vs PHI	3	7:45	1	9	PHI 9	9
Week 13 vs PHI	4	15:00	2	3	PHI 40	3
Week 17 vs CHI	1	7:27	1	10	GNB 20	-1

The Packers will run Outside Zone Strong – Lead, but not as often as a team like the 49ers. It is part of their system, but they do not hang their hat on it.

There are a myriad of ways to run this concept, but since it is a small piece of the Packers offense, they focus on the version where the fullback blocks the strong safety, or the first off ball defender. The next image shows this concept against an Over front.

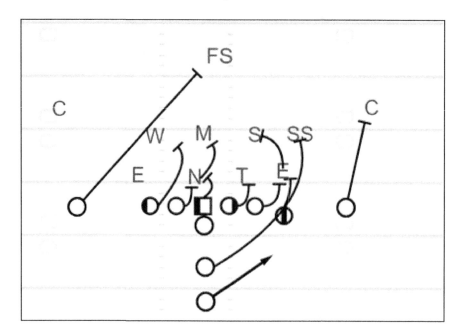

If a safety is rolled down to the weak side of the formation, the fullback will lead up on the Sam or Mike, depending on the call. Typically with a safety rolled down weak, the Sam is lined up on the ball in an Under or Bear front. The Packers most often had the tight end take the Sam on the ball, and the fullback take the Mike. This is shown in the next diagram.

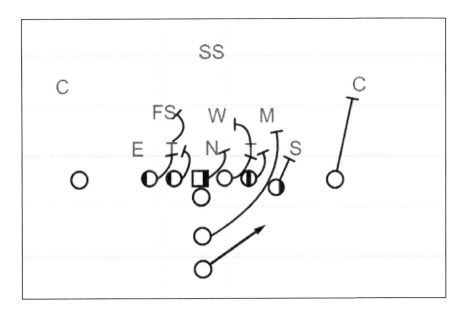

Occasionally the Packers would have the PSWR crack the strong safety and have the fullback lead out to the corner. A nice changeup to create better angles on the edge. This adjustment works even better when paired with the jet version, as the running back will have an easier time blocking the corner than fighting through traffic for a linebacker or safety.

This section includes variations of Outside Zone Strong – Lead out of 11 personnel with jet action, using the running back as the fullback. Using this concept with jet motion helps the offensive line get better angles to the second level, as the defense might not adjust fast enough.

With the addition of a lead blocker, the need to check out of this run into a different run or pass is mitigated. This can be a "call it – run it" play.

Why it Worked: The 2nd clip in week 7, the Williams cuts it back against an under Sam-up front. Williams presses it hard front side forcing the linebackers to over pursue.

Why it Didn't Work: There seems to be some confusion in the week 4 clip. The O-Line and fullback both work up to the Sam linebacker, leaving the Mike free to make the play in the backfield. The backside of the O-line works to the Will, which leads me to believe the fullback should have blocked the Mike.

Inside Zone Weak (11/12)

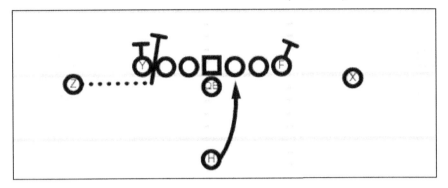

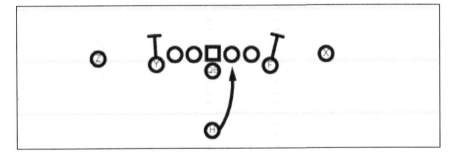

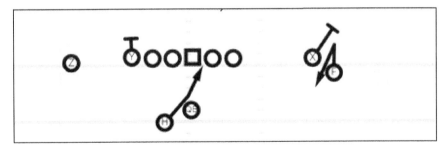

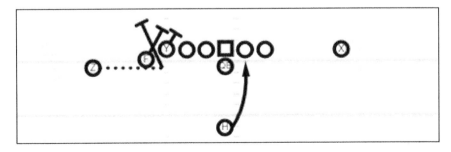

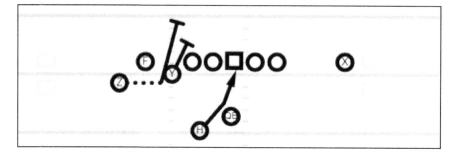

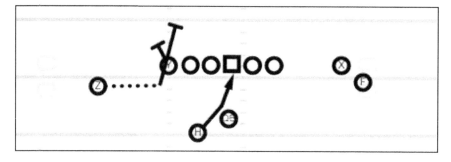

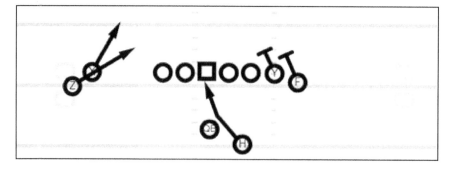

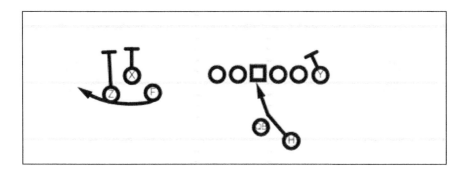

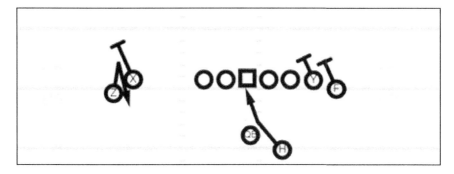

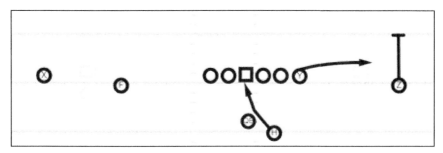

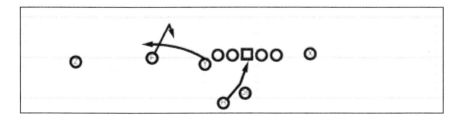

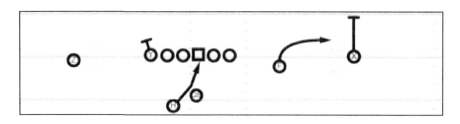

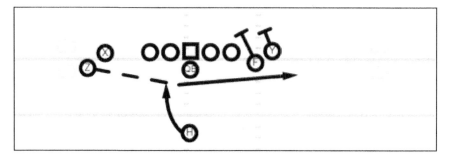

Average Yards per Play	6.2

1st Down		3rd/4th Down (includes RZ)	
Called	Average	Called	Success Rate
65	6.9	15	90%
2nd Down 6-1		2nd Down 7+	
Called	Average	Called	Average
21	4.4	18	8.7
Red Zone 10-0		Red Zone 10-20	
Called	Touchdown %	Called	Touchdown %
24	38%	9	0%

Bear		Over		6-Man	
Called	Average	Called	Average	Called	Average
21	3.2	66	7.0	7	0.9
Under (4 Man)		Mug		Under Sam Up	
Called	Average	Called	Average	Called	Average
1	7.0	2	5.0	11	8.8
Wide		Odd		Diamond	
Called	Average	Called	Average	Called	Average
7	14.7	4	4.0	0	0.0

Week	Quarter	Time	Down	ToGo	Location	Yards
Week 1 vs MN	2	2:00	2	6	MIN 33	0
Week 1 vs MN	2	0:47	2	9	MIN 24	24
Week 1 vs MN	3	11:21	2	2	GNB 17	1
Week 1 vs MN	4	13:53	1	10	GNB 25	8
Week 1 vs MN	4	4:53	1	10	MIN 23	6
Week 1 vs MN	4	3:24	1	5	MIN 5	5
Week 2 vs DET	1	10:29	1	10	GNB 25	12
Week 2 vs DET	1	9:47	1	10	GNB 37	4
Week 2 vs DET	2	11:39	1	10	DET 14	5
Week 2 vs DET	2	4:49	1	10	GNB 29	4
Week 2 vs DET	3	15:00	1	10	GNB 25	75
Week 2 vs DET	3	13:09	1	10	GNB 21	18
Week 2 vs DET	3	2:38	2	6	DET 26	4
Week 2 vs DET	4	11:45	2	11	GNB 25	7
Week 2 vs DET	4	10:08	1	10	DET 27	1
Week 2 vs DET	4	9:24	2	9	DET 26	3
Week 2 vs DET	4	5:26	2	7	GNB 39	3
Week 3 vs NO	3	13:54	2	3	NOR 3	2
Week 3 vs NO	3	13:01	4	1	NOR 1	1
Week 3 vs NO	4	4:34	2	5	NOR 17	2
Week 3 vs NO	4	2:52	1	1	NOR 1	0
Week 4 vs ATL	1	3:19	4	1	ATL 1	0
Week 4 vs ATL	2	1:37	1	10	GNB 50	5
Week 4 vs ATL	3	6:07	2	4	ATL 22	1
Week 4 vs ATL	4	10:46	1	10	GNB 48	3
Week 4 vs ATL	4	2:32	2	11	ATL 46	2
Week 6 vs TB	3	11:42	2	6	GNB 29	1
Week 6 vs TB	3	7:50	1	10	GNB 34	7
Week 6 vs TB	4	12:07	1	10	GNB 12	3

Week	Quarter	Time	Down	ToGo	Location	Yards
Week 7 vs HOU	1	7:10	2	10	GNB 20	2
Week 7 vs HOU	1	3:10	1	10	GNB 12	2
Week 7 vs HOU	1	2:01	1	10	GNB 22	0
Week 7 vs HOU	3	8:55	1	10	GNB 25	6
Week 7 vs HOU	3	3:52	1	10	GNB 24	0
Week 7 vs HOU	4	13:27	2	7	GNB 29	6
Week 7 vs HOU	4	3:43	1	1	HTX 1	1
Week 8 vs MIN	2	14:18	3	1	GNB 37	3
Week 8 vs MIN	2	7:38	4	1	MIN 8	1
Week 8 vs MIN	2	0:25	1	10	GNB 29	8
Week 8 vs MIN	4	5:47	1	10	GNB 26	5
Week 8 vs MIN	4	2:41			MIN 2	2
Week 9 vs SF	1	12:22	1	10	SFO 38	2
Week 9 vs SF	2	5:22	2	10	GNB 13	5
Week 9 vs SF	2	4:59	1	10	GNB 23	3
Week 9 vs SF	2	3:09	1	10	GNB 35	2
Week 9 vs SF	3	13:17	1	10	GNB 20	3
Week 9 vs SF	3	3:33	1	10	SFO 10	7
Week 9 vs SF	4	8:29	1	15	SFO 35	0
Week 10 vs JAX	1	15:00	1	10	GNB 25	5
Week 10 vs JAX	1	5:02	1	10	GNB 4	1
Week 10 vs JAX	2	5:15	3	1	JAX 31	1
Week 10 vs JAX	3	9:18	2	10	GNB 43	2
Week 10 vs JAX	3	2:03	2	10	JAX 49	2
Week 10 vs JAX	4	9:49	1	10	JAX 24	18
Week 11 vs IND	2	12:41	2	5	CLT 35	4
Week 11 vs IND	2	7:52	1	5	CLT 5	5
Week 11 vs IND	2	1:48	2	5	GNB 30	4
Week 11 vs IND	2	1:05	3	1	GNB 34	2
Week 12 vs CHI	1	10:20	1	10	CHI 25	8
Week 12 vs CHI	2	0:11	1	10	GNB 35	3
Week 12 vs CHI	3	10:26	3	20	GNB 24	0
Week 12 vs CHI	3	8:45	1	10	GNB 47	4
Week 12 vs CHI	3	7:23	1	10	CHI 41	2
Week 12 vs CHI	3	4:47	1	10	CHI 42	17
Week 12 vs CHI	3	4:07	1	10	CHI 25	4
Week 12 vs CHI	3	3:25	2	6	CHI 21	4
Week 12 vs CHI	3	1:59	4	1	CHI 16	3
Week 12 vs CHI	4	3:13	2	10	CHI 47	1

Week	Quarter	Time	Down	ToGo	Location	Yards
Week 13 vs PHI	2	15:00	1	10	GNB 37	5
Week 13 vs PHI	2	8:33	4	1	PHI 1	1
Week 13 vs PHI	3	3:35	1	10	GNB 6	18
Week 13 vs PHI	4	13:36	2	7	PHI 34	8
Week 13 vs PHI	4	5:45	2	9	GNB 23	-1
Week 13 vs PHI	4	2:51	2	7	GNB 23	77
Week 13 vs PHI	4	1:47	1	10	GNB 34	1
Week 14 vs DET	1	1:32	1	10	DET 37	5
Week 14 vs DET	2	8:35	2	4	GNB 39	4
Week 14 vs DET	2	1:18	2	2	GNB 31	4
Week 14 vs DET	3	9:06	1	10	DET 21	0
Week 14 vs DET	3	7:04	2	10	DET 10	4
Week 14 vs DET	4	15:00	2	2	DET 26	9
Week 14 vs DET	4	14:19	1	10	DET 17	7
Week 14 vs DET	4	13:30	2	3	DET 10	2
Week 14 vs DET	4	5:52	2	3	GNB 32	7
Week 15 vs CAR	1	5:13	2	8	GNB 27	1
Week 15 vs CAR	1	1:44	3	1	CAR 46	14
Week 15 vs CAR	2	15:00	1	10	CAR 10	4
Week 15 vs CAR	2	4:42	1	10	CAR 13	5
Week 15 vs CAR	4	8:09	1	10	GNB 35	5
Week 16 vs TEN	2	11:28	3	3	OTI 13	6
Week 16 vs TEN	2	8:14	1	10	OTI 32	2
Week 16 vs TEN	2	6:45	3	3	OTI 25	6
Week 16 vs TEN	3	5:11	2	2	OTI 31	1
Week 16 vs TEN	3	3:42	4	1	OTI 30	30
Week 16 vs TEN	4	2:30	2	7	OTI 7	7
Week 17 vs CHI	2	4:49	1	17	CHI 17	4
Week 17 vs CHI	4	9:51	1	10	GNB 37	3
Week 17 vs CHI	4	3:50	1	4	CHI 4	4
Week 17 vs CHI	4	3:13	1	10	CHI 26	6

Week	Quarter	Time	Down	ToGo	Location	Yards
DIV vs LAR	1	13:25	1	10	GNB 32	2
DIV vs LAR	1	9:27	1	4	RAM 4	-1
DIV vs LAR	1	3:10	3	1	GNB 25	8
DIV vs LAR	2	15:00	1	10	RAM 39	3
DIV vs LAR	2	13:06	1	9	RAM 9	3
DIV vs LAR	2	12:23	2	6	RAM 6	5
DIV vs LAR	2	11:40	3	1	RAM 1	1
DIV vs LAR	2	5:33	3	2	RAM 13	5
DIV vs LAR	2	5:00	1	8	RAM 8	4
DIV vs LAR	2	4:22	2	4	RAM 4	3
DIV vs LAR	3	15:00	1	10	GNB 25	60
DIV vs LAR	3	12:52	1	3	RAM 3	2
DIV vs LAR	3	1:36	1	10	GNB 26	4
DIV vs LAR	4	14:20	1	10	GNB 50	3
NFCCG vs TB	1	1:09	1	10	GNB 28	15
NFCCG vs TB	2	6:44	2	9	TAM 17	7
NFCCG vs TB	3	13:16	2	4	GNB 31	1
NFCCG vs TB	3	7:06	2	3	GNB 39	4
NFCCG vs TB	3	3:44	2	5	TAM 27	3
NFCCG vs TB	3	1:13	1	2	TAM 2	0
NFCCG vs TB	4	4:33	1	10	GNB 34	9

In a 12 personnel Y-Wing alignment, the offense has the ability to use both tight ends to double the back side defensive end up to the 2nd level. If a defensive end gives your tight end trouble in a 1 on 1 cutoff block on the back side of inside zone, adding a second tight end can help mitigate this problem.

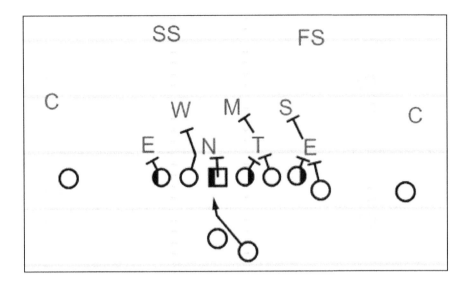

Against single high defense, LaFleur will often incorporate short motion from his Z receiver (or across motion if lined up in a nub formation) to block the strong safety. Similar to the Duo concept, this allows the offense to block all of the box defenders at the point of attack. The next image shows this action out of 12 personnel.

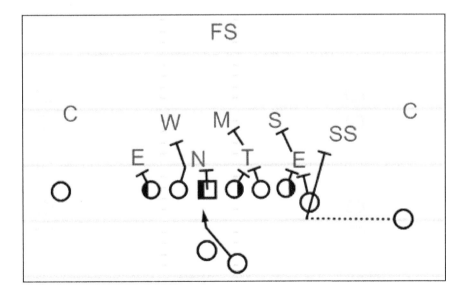

The Duo section shows what this block looks like in 11 personnel against a wide 9 defensive end. The receiver will insert inside of the tight end's block for the strong safety.

Many of the RPO variations call for the run play and the pass concept to the same side of the field. This is an adjustment specifically to attack defenses that like to add an extra run fitter (usually out of two high) to the side the quarterback turns his back to. A great example of this defensive tactic can be seen in week 1 2Q 1:17. Zimmer and the Vikings slant their defensive end inside to steal a gap back out of two high, and have the nickel fall into the front side C-gap. The next diagram shows how this scheme gets numbers back for the defense in the run game.

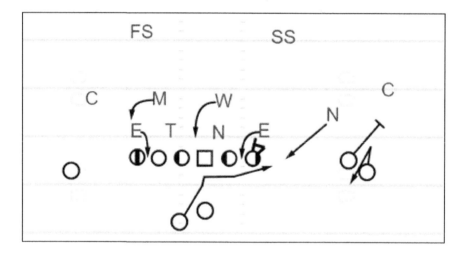

Because of the initial alignment of the nickel over #2 and the timing of the delayed reaction to the run, Rodgers is not able to read the RPO pre-snap correctly to get the ball to Adams on the outside for a 2 on 1 on the now screen. These RPO's are hard to read post-snap with he quarterback having his back turned to the action. The decision to throw the Now is typically made pre-snap based on alignment.

A good example of Rodgers correctly identifying this pre-snap can be seen in week 7 early 4Q. With the slot defender mid-pointing pre-snap, Rodgers has a good indication that he is the conflict defender. With the inside zone action coming towards him, his responsibility is to fall into he run fit out of two high, leaving the Now screen in a 2 on 1.

The 8th diagram shows a red zone RPO used in week 3. If the offense gets a goal line defense with man coverage on the outside, Rodgers can sling the ball out to the shield slant.

The 2x2 TE Arrow RPO shown in the 11th diagram is a creative way for the offense to get a 2 for 1 on the backside. The Arrow route will influence both the flat defender and the defensive end. The Packers do not want Aaron Rodgers reading the back side defensive end on zone read. This version is a nice way to get around the read while still not having to block the defensive end. There are examples of the running back hitting the back side C-gap on this version throughout 2019 and 2020. The next image shows the cutback lane created. Against wide 9 fronts, this lane is intensified.

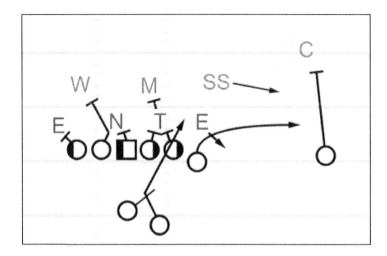

The 12th diagram shows an RPO used on 4th down in week 12 vs Chicago. Against man coverage the TE should open up with the pick from the slot receiver.

Why it Worked: In week 13, the Eagles bring the safety off the front side of the run and slant the line back. The tight ends do a nice job sealing the wide-9 and off ball Sam for a big cutback lane.

In week 12, the Bears try to steal a gap back out of two high by slanting the play side 5 technique into the B gap. Aaron Jones has his head up and does a nice job of recognizing this and bounces the run front side. You won't see this too often with inside zone at the NFL level.

The Packers get some big plays from this concept in week 2 vs Detroit's cover 2 shell. The extra double teams and good angles to the second level gave this play a little extra juice in this game.

The Packers had a nice conversion rate with inside zone on third and fourth downs. This shows the ability to get a quick jump off the line of scrimmage and get a good initial push.

Why it Didn't Work: On 3rd & 2 in week 10, Valdez-Scantling has the insert block on the strong safety. He does not use his motion well to set up the angle and lines up too wide. The strong safety knifes through and makes the tackle in the backfield.

Inside Zone Slice (11/12)

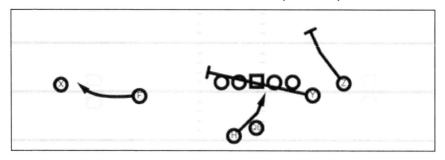

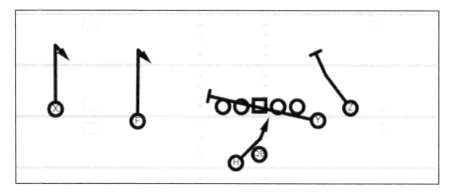

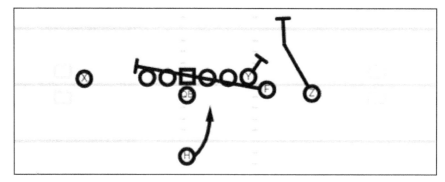

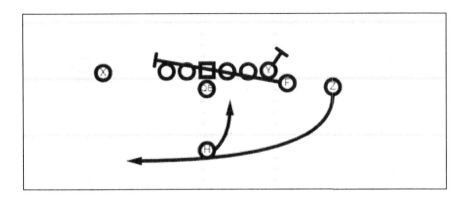

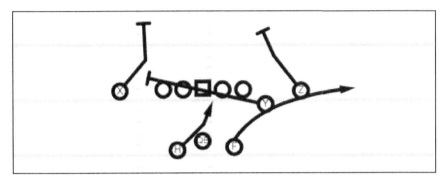

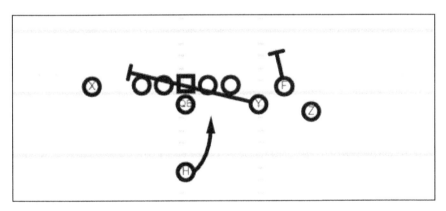

Average Yards per Play	5.7

1st Down		3rd/4th Down (includes RZ)	
Called	Average	Called	Success Rate
20	6.8	1	0%
2nd Down 6-1		**2nd Down 7+**	
Called	Average	Called	Average
4	16.8	3	2.3
Red Zone 10-0		**Red Zone 10-20**	
Called	Touchdown %	Called	Touchdown %
5	20%	1	0%

Bear		Over		6-Man	
Called	Average	Called	Average	Called	Average
3	2.7	17	9.8	0	0.0
Under (4 Man)		**Mug**		**Under Sam Up**	
Called	Average	Called	Average	Called	Average
2	4.0	1	2.0	2	5.0
Wide		**Odd**		**Diamond**	
Called	Average	Called	Average	Called	Average
2	8.0	2	4.5	0	0.0

Week	Quarter	Time	Down	ToGo	Location	Yards
Week 3 vs NO	1	13:08	1	10	GNB 31	4
Week 3 vs NO	4	5:59	1	10	NOR 41	19
Week 4 vs ATL	2	4:35	1	10	ATL 33	3
Week 6 vs TB	1	11:27	1	10	TAM 23	0
Week 6 vs TB	3	6:27	2	10	GNB 45	2
Week 7 vs HOU	1	15:00	1	10	GNB 25	3
Week 7 vs HOU	1	13:18	1	10	GNB 38	5
Week 7 vs HOU	1	2:01	1	10	GNB 22	0
Week 7 vs HOU	1	0:07	1	10	HTX 49	8
Week 7 vs HOU	2	14:23	1	5	HTX 5	2
Week 7 vs HOU	2	8:11	2	6	HTX 48	4
Week 7 vs HOU	2	1:28	2	4	HTX 32	9
Week 7 vs HOU	2	0:30	1	8	HTX 8	7
Week 7 vs HOU	4	14:07	1	10	GNB 26	3
Week 7 vs HOU	4	6:58	1	10	HTX 46	4
Week 7 vs HOU	4	5:33	1	10	HTX 33	-2
Week 8 vs MIN	1	7:45	2	7	MIN 8	3
Week 8 vs MIN	2	10:56	1	10	MIN 31	2
Week 9 vs SF	4	14:29	1	10	GNB 5	3
Week 11 vs IND	2	9:59	1	2	CLT 2	2
Week 14 vs DET	2	9:16	1	10	GNB 33	6
Week 15 vs CAR	4	4:31	2	8	CAR 27	2
Week 16 vs TEN	3	11:57	1	10	GNB 34	59
Week 17 vs CHI	1	1:16	3	5	CHI 25	2
Week 17 vs CHI	1	0:29	1	7	CHI 7	4
DIV vs LAR	4	15:00	2	3	GNB 46	4
NFCCG vs TB	2	15:00	2	5	GNB 48	2
NFCCG vs TB	2	2:10	1	10	GNB 13	0

Against over fronts, 11 personnel split zone is a nice way to create the back side C-gap cutback lane.

Out of a condensed formation, the wide receivers on each side would dig out any safety or nickel in the run fit. Although this leaves the corner unblocked, the Packers are now able to block all of the box defenders. This is common in Green Bay's run game with outside zone and duo concepts as well.

Against 5 man fronts, the addition of a second tight end can add an extra double team on the back side. The next section (Inside Zone Slice – Fake Jet) discusses this and draws it out.

In this section, the Packers saw looks where the second tight end would not necessarily add a double team, so they would tag him on an arrow route to influence the EMOL and a 2nd level support player. In the next diagram, a down block from the tight end would not add a double team, so the arrow tag will influence two defenders out of the box.

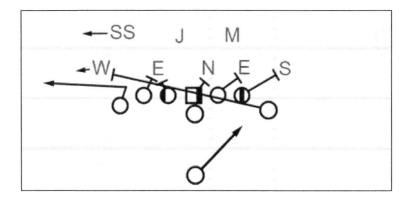

Why it Worked: In week 3 4Q, the Saints stunt and clog up the zone combos which prevents the slicer from getting to the back side defensive end. This block did not matter on this play because the defensive end flew so far up field, Jones was able to cutback in the C-gap regardless for a nice gain.

Why it Didn't Work: The 2Q NFCCG clip shows the need for condensed receiver splits on this concept. The Bucs bring a secondary blitz off the front side, and the Packers do not have someone to account for him because the Z receiver is split out wide. Additionally, the under-front nose slants across the center's face to disrupt the play too.

Inside Zone Slice – Fake Jet (11/12)

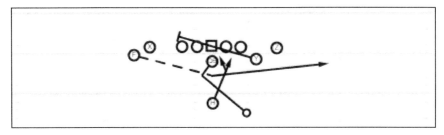

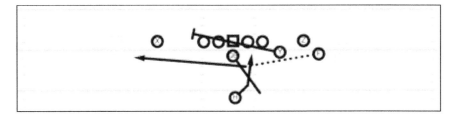

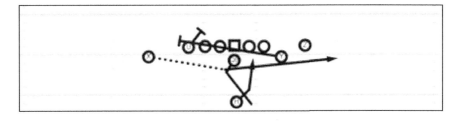

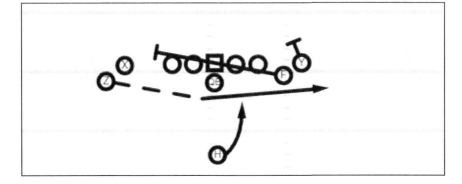

Average Yards per Play	4.3

1st Down		3rd/4th Down (includes RZ)	
Called	Average	Called	Success Rate
11	4.1	1	0%
2nd Down 6-1		**2nd Down 7+**	
Called	Average	Called	Average
3	3.0	2	10.0
Red Zone 10-0		**Red Zone 10-20**	
Called	Touchdown %	Called	Touchdown %
5	20%	3	0%

Bear		Over		6-Man	
Called	Average	Called	Average	Called	Average
3	1.3	5	5.6	2	0.5
Under (4 Man)		**Mug**		**Under Sam Up**	
Called	Average	Called	Average	Called	Average
2	5.5	0	0.0	3	5.0
Wide		**Odd**		**Diamond**	
Called	Average	Called	Average	Called	Average
1	14.0	2	1.5	0	0.0

Week	Quarter	Time	Down	ToGo	Location	Yards
Week 1 vs MN	2	13:07	3	1	MIN 1	0
Week 1 vs MN	3	1:00	1	2	MIN 2	1
Week 2 vs DET	4	7:59			DET 2	2
Week 3 vs NO	1	3:52	2	5	GNB 40	4
Week 4 vs ATL	1	10:44	1	6	ATL 6	0
Week 6 vs TB	1	6:07	1	10	GNB 34	25
Week 6 vs TB	2	4:35	1	10	GNB 25	7
Week 6 vs TB	3	2:40	1	10	GNB 25	-3
Week 7 vs HOU	1	10:50	1	8	HTX 8	5
Week 9 vs SF	4	11:43	2	2	SFO 47	4
Week 12 vs CHI	1	14:17	2	10	GNB 36	14
Week 12 vs CHI	1	1:25	1	10	CHI 18	2
Week 13 vs PHI	2	10:59	2	4	PHI 18	1
Week 14 vs DET	1	3:39	1	10	DET 48	3
Week 17 vs CHI	4	5:23	1	10	CHI 19	1
DIV vs LAR	1	3:50	2	7	GNB 19	6
DIV vs LAR	2	14:33	1	10	RAM 21	4
NFCCG vs TB	1	9:44	1	10	GNB 42	1

The fake jet motion provides the same benefits it does for the other concepts in the Packers offense. It forces the defense to adjust their run fits on the fly and forces communication errors. Depending if the jet motion goes to the call or away from the call will have different effects on the second level defenders as well. The second diagram forces the nickel to fit an interior run gap if the defense chooses to bump with he motion and fall back with the slicer.

The third diagram shows a variation used twice in week 12 against Chicago. Against odd & 5-man over/under fronts, having the extra tight end allows for the back side defensive end to be double teamed. The in-line tight end can down block with the BST, and the Slicer will handle the outside linebacker. The play is drawn up in the next diagram

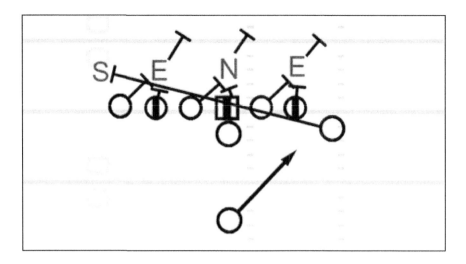

Without the in-line tight end, the BST would have the head up 4 technique on his own.

Why it Worked: In week 6,the center and BST are able to get up to the Bucs speedy linebackers quickly. The play hits front side A gap for a big gain.

Why it Didn't Work: In week 17, Williams feels the safety blitz off the back side and prematurely hits the front side A gap. The nose does a nice job of two gapping the center on this play too.

Duo (11)

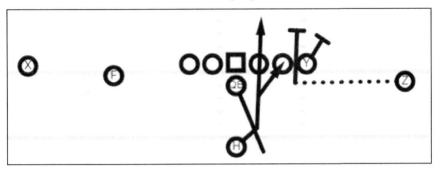

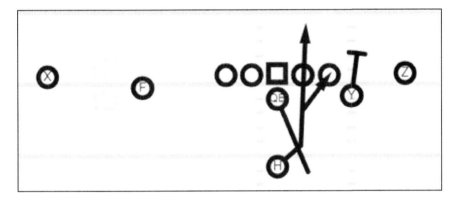

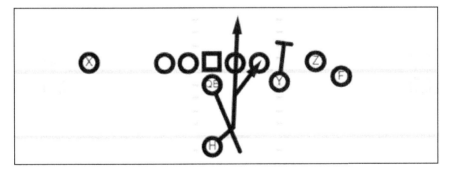

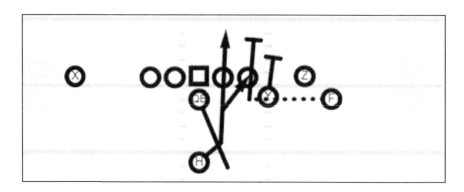

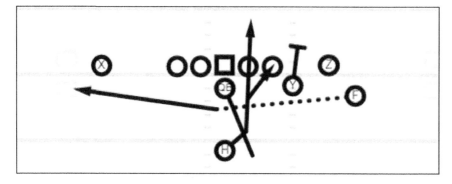

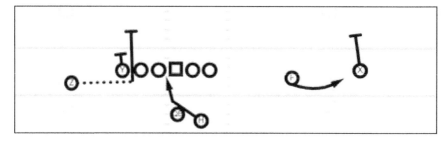

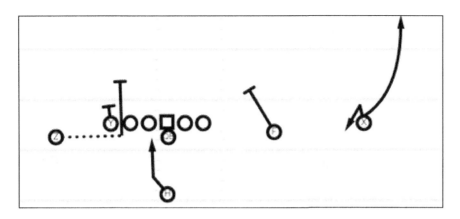

Average Yards per Play	5.6

1st Down		3rd/4th Down (includes RZ)	
Called	Average	Called	Success Rate
13	5.8	4	33%
2nd Down 6-1		**2nd Down 7+**	
Called	Average	Called	Average
14	6.5	6	2.0
Red Zone 10-0		**Red Zone 10-20**	
Called	Touchdown %	Called	Touchdown %
8	50%	3	33%

Bear		Over		6-Man	
Called	Average	Called	Average	Called	Average
6	8.3	22	5.7	1	0.0
Under (4 Man)		**Mug**		**Under Sam Up**	
Called	Average	Called	Average	Called	Average
6	4.5	0	0.0	0	0.0
Wide		**Odd**		**Diamond**	
Called	Average	Called	Average	Called	Average
0	0.0	1	9.0	1	-3.0

Week	Quarter	Time	Down	ToGo	Location	Yards
Week 1 vs MN	4	11:50	2	7	MIN 43	0
Week 1 vs MN	4	10:09	2	4	MIN 4	4
Week 3 vs NO	3	15:00	1	10	GNB 25	0
Week 3 vs NO	3	14:54	2	10	GNB 25	0
Week 3 vs NO	3	5:15	1	10	GNB 41	5
Week 3 vs NO	3	3:09	2	5	NOR 21	3
Week 4 vs ATL	3	14:08	2	8	GNB 23	2
Week 7 vs HOU	3	6:18	2	5	GNB 44	5
Week 7 vs HOU	4	12:53	3	1	GNB 35	-3
Week 7 vs HOU	4	4:48	2	12	HTX 35	5
Week 9 vs SF	3	2:55	2	3	SFO 3	2
Week 10 vs JAX	1	14:25	2	5	GNB 30	2
Week 10 vs JAX	2	12:32	1	10	GNB 27	-3
Week 10 vs JAX	3	8:49	1	10	JAX 40	5
Week 11 vs IND	2	14:09	1	10	GNB 40	20
Week 12 vs CHI	1	4:40	2	2	GNB 33	3
Week 12 vs CHI	2	8:12	2	6	CHI 32	2
Week 12 vs CHI	2	5:23	2	5	CHI 9	7
Week 12 vs CHI	3	5:28	2	10	GNB 34	0
Week 12 vs CHI	3	5:22	3	10	GNB 34	24
Week 12 vs CHI	3	1:18	1	10	CHI 13	13
Week 12 vs CHI	4	11:48	1	10	GNB 25	2
Week 12 vs CHI	4	3:01	4	2	CHI 39	8
Week 12 vs CHI	4	2:00	2	6	CHI 27	10
Week 13 vs PHI	2	8:36	3	1	PHI 1	0
Week 13 vs PHI	3	8:30	2	3	PHI 12	3
Week 13 vs PHI	3	0:32	1	10	PHI 47	7
Week 13 vs PHI	4	1:43	2	9	GNB 35	5
Week 14 vs DET	1	9:24	1	10	GNB 25	4
Week 14 vs DET	4	1:44	2	6	DET 41	1
Week 15 vs CAR	2	4:04	2	5	CAR 8	8
Week 16 vs TEN	1	9:59	1	5	OTI 5	5
Week 16 vs TEN	2	10:49	1	7	OTI 7	7
Week 16 vs TEN	4	6:11	2	1	GNB 32	27
Week 16 vs TEN	4	3:14	1	9	OTI 9	2
Week 17 vs CHI	3	5:30	1	10	GNB 25	9
Week 17 vs CHI	4	3:08	2	4	CHI 20	14

Duo is a NFL-Staple downhill run. Many coaches define Duo and Inside Zone differently, so let's define the difference for the purpose of this book. Duo runs are differentiated based on the aiming point of the running back. If he starts in the strong A gap (towards the tight end), I defined it as Duo. When the running back works to press the weak A gap, it is defined as inside zone. Both schemes allow for bounce/cutback towards the tight end.

Duo is characterized by strong double teams. The offensive line is working to get vertical movement working to the will linebacker. The running back will read the fit of the middle linebacker. If he fits downhill, the running back will often bounce the play outside the tight end. If he chooses to play it over the top, the running back should stick his foot in the ground and hit the play vertically downhill.

The play side corner is often unblocked against single high defenses. This allows the offense to block the most dangerous defenders while not sacrificing poor angles for the double team to linebacker combos. The Z receiver will dig out the strong safety. The diagram below shows the concept against a base Over Cover 3.

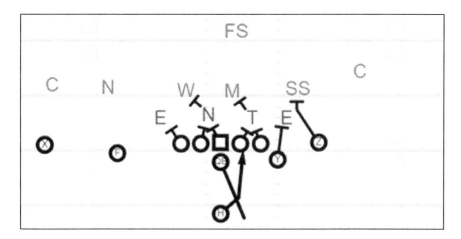

Against this front, the tight end is asked to block the defensive end 1 on 1. Marcedes Lewis is a great personnel fit for this play, as he does a great job with these blocks.

Against defenses with a wide-9 defensive end, or with the strong safety tucked in the box, short motion is used the help the Z receiver get a better angle on his block. The next image shows this adjustment.

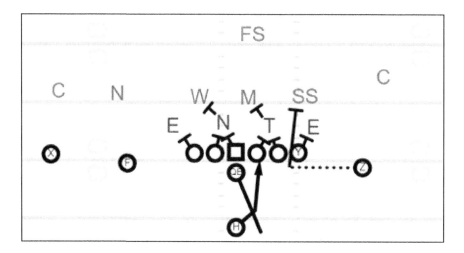

This was used frequently against teams like Chicago, who base out of an odd front. When in 11 personnel, the Packers often force these defenses into a four down front. With both outside linebackers on the field, they typically line up wider and play the edge instead of the strong safety in a base four down front. The short motion was also used often against the Eagles Wide-9 Over front for the same purpose.

The 2nd clip in week 7 shows Rodgers adjusting the play and alignment of the Z receiver against cover two. Against cover two, the offense wants a big split from the Z to keep the low corner out of the run fit.

Why it Worked: On the big run in week 12, the Bears play cover two and do not have a player to fit the front side A gap. Williams reads the middle linebacker fit the back side

A gap and hits the front side A vertically.

The 7th diagram shows an under-center RPO used in week 16 in the red zone. Adams scored twice on this concept, once on the quick now throw and once on the fade.

Why it Didn't Work: In week 14 at the end of the game, the Lions crowd their linebackers at the line of scrimmage and trigger them at the snap. This takes away the ability for the offense to double team and forces 1 on 1 matchups at the snap.

Duo (12)

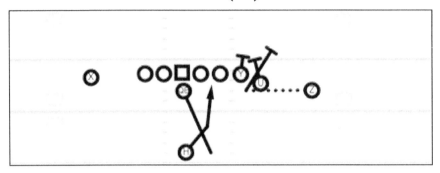

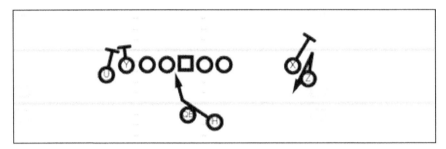

Average Yards per Play	3.8

1st Down		3rd/4th Down (includes RZ)	
Called	Average	Called	Success Rate
24	4.7	1	0%
2nd Down 6-1		**2nd Down 7+**	
Called	Average	Called	Average
7	4.3	3	0.0
Red Zone 10-0		**Red Zone 10-20**	
Called	Touchdown %	Called	Touchdown %
2	0%	3	0%

Bear		Over		6-Man	
Called	Average	Called	Average	Called	Average
6	4.3	12	4.2	2	6.0
Under (4 Man)		Mug		Under Sam Up	
Called	Average	Called	Average	Called	Average
1	4.0	2	3.0	7	3.6
Wide		Odd		Diamond	
Called	Average	Called	Average	Called	Average
0	0.0	4	5.8	0	0.0

Week	Quarter	Time	Down	ToGo	Location	Yards
Week 1 vs MN	2	13:27	1	3	MIN 3	2
Week 2 vs DET	3	6:53	1	10	GNB 25	3
Week 2 vs DET	4	2:00	2	11	DET 41	0
Week 3 vs NO	3	4:40	2	5	GNB 46	9
Week 4 vs ATL	1	4:49	2	3	ATL 3	0
Week 4 vs ATL	4	11:32	2	4	GNB 42	6
Week 6 vs TB	2	11:02	1	10	GNB 25	0
Week 7 vs HOU	2	8:52	1	10	GNB 48	4
Week 9 vs SF	4	7:45	2	15	SFO 35	0
Week 9 vs SF	4	5:00	1	10	GNB 25	2
Week 9 vs SF	4	4:16	2	8	GNB 27	0
Week 9 vs SF	4	3:33	3	8	GNB 27	4
Week 12 vs CHI	1	3:12	1	10	CHI 34	5
Week 13 vs PHI	3	11:14	1	10	GNB 43	6
Week 13 vs PHI	4	14:21	1	10	PHI 37	3
Week 14 vs DET	1	5:43	1	10	GNB 41	3
Week 14 vs DET	3	0:27	1	10	DET 34	8
Week 15 vs CAR	3	15:00	1	10	GNB 25	3
Week 15 vs CAR	4	2:04	1	10	GNB 25	7
Week 15 vs CAR	4	1:58	2	3	GNB 32	-1
Week 16 vs TEN	3	8:06	2	2	GNB 45	6
Week 16 vs TEN	4	5:32	1	10	OTI 41	0
Week 17 vs CHI	4	6:53	1	10	CHI 40	4
DIV vs LAR	1	4:29	1	10	GNB 16	3
DIV vs LAR	2	7:21	1	10	RAM 21	6
DIV vs LAR	3	9:15	1	10	GNB 29	11
DIV vs LAR	4	9:46	1	10	GNB 27	6
DIV vs LAR	4	4:59	1	10	RAM 46	1
DIV vs LAR	4	3:26	1	10	RAM 33	6
DIV vs LAR	4	2:42	2	4	RAM 27	6
DIV vs LAR	4	2:35	1	10	RAM 21	8
DIV vs LAR	4	2:30	2	2	RAM 13	4
NFCCG vs TB	2	7:26	1	10	TAM 18	1
NFCCG vs TB	3	5:52	1	10	TAM 44	5
NFCCG vs TB	3	2:23	1	10	TAM 13	1

Similar to the zone schemes, the two tight end look for Duo allows the offense to get a double team on the play side defensive end. The double teams work very similar to the inside zone scheme.

With a 3x1 presentation, the defense will most often roll the strong safety down to get to a single high look (in lieu of rolling weak). Strong rotation will require the offense to use the Z receiver to block the down safety, often needing short motion to get him a better angle. Allen Lazard is great at this block and many of the clips can be used as teach tape for this block.

Against a wide-9 defensive end or where the safety is up near the line of scrimmage, the Z receiver will often have to motion inside the tight ends to create a better angle for the block. Occasionally, as explained in the Duo (11) section, he will have to insert inside the tight end to make the block.

This scheme is often used late in games to run out the clock.

Why it Worked: The first clip in week 16 shows Lazard washing down the strong safety fitting the E-gap outside the 2nd TE, springing AJ Dillon onto the corner 1 on 1 in the open field. This Duo scheme is a good fit for AJ Dillon as he is quite a load for a corner having to tackle.

In week 3, Aaron Jones is able to hit the play vertically down hill while staying outside the tight ends. The unblocked corner has to make the tackle ten yards downfield.

Why it Didn't Work: Using heavy bear or mug fronts allow defenses to eliminate double teams and force 1 on 1 blocks. Late in the game in week 15 the Panthers run a mug front and are able to get some push into he backfield.

Duo Wrap (11/12)

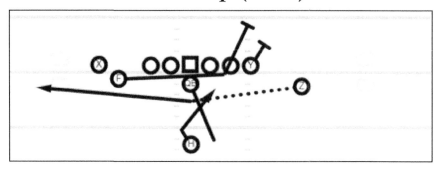

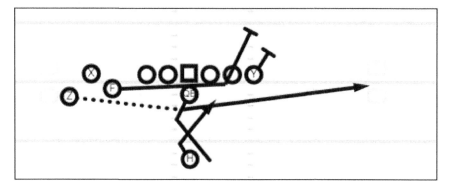

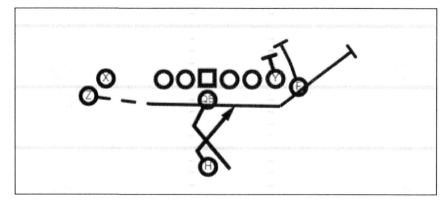

Average Yards per Play	4.7

1st Down		3rd/4th Down (includes RZ)	
Called	Average	Called	Success Rate
9	4.0	2	0%
2nd Down 6-1		**2nd Down 7+**	
Called	Average	Called	Average
1	9.0	3	5.7
Red Zone 10-0		**Red Zone 10-20**	
Called	Touchdown %	Called	Touchdown %
0	0%	3	0%

Bear		Over		6-Man	
Called	Average	Called	Average	Called	Average
5	5.0	8	4.1	0	0.0
Under (4 Man)		**Mug**		**Under Sam Up**	
Called	Average	Called	Average	Called	Average
0	0.0	0	0.0	0	0.0
Wide		**Odd**		**Diamond**	
Called	Average	Called	Average	Called	Average
0	0.0	0	0.0	0	0.0

Week	Quarter	Time	Down	ToGo	Location	Yards
Week 8 vs MIN	1	0:41	1	10	GNB 28	7
Week 8 vs MIN	3	5:48	2	10	GNB 25	5
Week 9 vs SF	1	9:23	2	8	GNB 22	9
Week 9 vs SF	2	8:34	1	10	SFO 14	3
Week 10 vs JAX	2	7:54	1	10	GNB 45	3
Week 12 vs CHI	1	11:02	2	5	CHI 34	9
Week 12 vs CHI	3	2:43	3	2	CHI 17	1
Week 12 vs CHI	4	3:09	3	9	CHI 46	7
Week 12 vs CHI	4	2:45	1	10	CHI 31	4
Week 13 vs PHI	3	14:42	2	10	GNB 33	3
Week 14 vs DET	1	5:43	1	10	GNB 41	3
Week 14 vs DET	2	15:00	1	10	DET 15	1
Week 14 vs DET	2	10:27	1	10	GNB 20	2
Week 16 vs TEN	4	6:59	1	10	GNB 23	9
Week 17 vs CHI	3	14:51	1	10	GNB 28	4

Duo Wrap is a nice misdirection changeup to traditional Duo. The wrapper will most often block the strong safety, usually the responsibility of the play side receiver. The blocking for the offensive line will remain the same.

The running back will use counter footwork with his action as well to add to the misdirection element.

The version in the first diagram, with the wrapper coming opposite the fake jet, is great for helping the offensive line. The fake jet going opposite pushes the linebackers the double teams are working to further away. This allows for longer double teams with better angles. The next diagram shows this playing out.

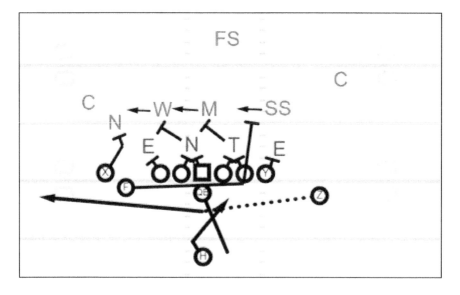

The variation in the 2nd diagram, with the fake jet and wrap going the same way, lends to the running back hitting the back side. The diagram below shows how the double teams will work more over the top. This gets the nickel in the back side B gap. Additionally, the linebackers have to double bump with the fast motion and the wrapper, with the fast motion, they often can miss the wrapper creating a +1 and not bump enough. The Rams run this often and have some good tape on the concept as well.

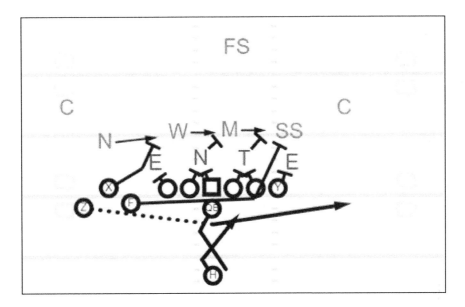

Why it Worked: In the 1st quarter of week 12, the Packers run the version shown in the 2nd diagram. The linebackers all bump twice, leaving the nickel in the back side B gap. The remaining receiver on the back side is able to get enough of him for a nice gain.

The touchdown run in week 12 was against a bear front with the middle linebacker blitzing front side A gap. The diagram below shows how the offensive line washes down the front and creates a nice lane for the running back.

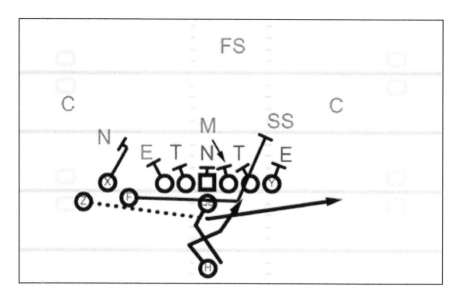

Why it Didn't Work: In week 14, the Mike does a nice job of recovering over the top. Jones reads this and cuts inside of the double-teamed 3 technique. The double team does not get any movement so the play is stopped at the line of scrimmage.

Power

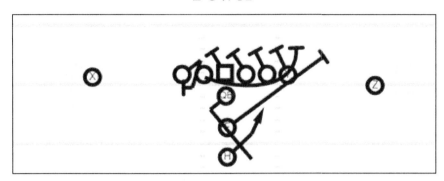

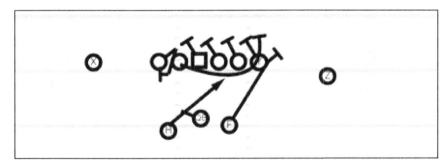

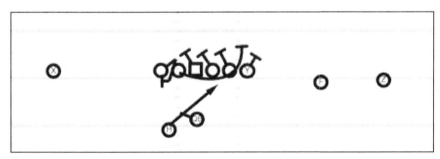

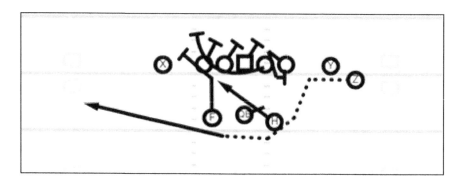

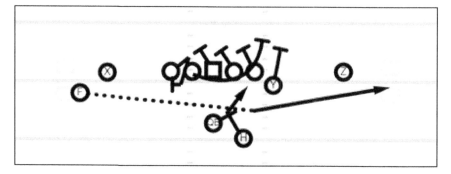

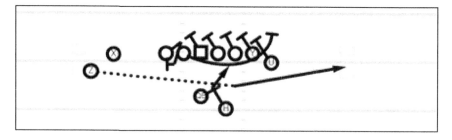

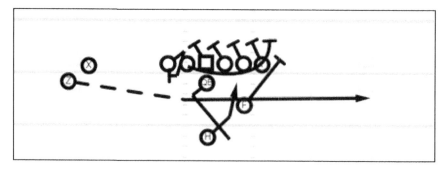

Average Yards per Play	6.4

1st Down		3rd/4th Down (includes RZ)	
Called	Average	Called	Success Rate
12	7.5	0	0%
2nd Down 6-1		2nd Down 7+	
Called	Average	Called	Average
5	3.2	4	7.3
Red Zone 10-0		Red Zone 10-20	
Called	Touchdown %	Called	Touchdown %
1	0%	3	0%

Bear		Over		6-Man	
Called	Average	Called	Average	Called	Average
2	3.0	13	7.2	0	0.0
Under (4 Man)		Mug		Under Sam Up	
Called	Average	Called	Average	Called	Average
0	0.0	0	0.0	1	4.0
Wide		Odd		Diamond	
Called	Average	Called	Average	Called	Average
0	0.0	3	6.7	0	0.0

Week	Quarter	Time	Down	ToGo	Location	Yards
Week 2 vs DET	1	9:10	2	6	GNB 41	-2
Week 3 vs NO	4	6:36	1	10	GNB 36	23
Week 4 vs ATL	1	11:28	1	10	ATL 29	23
Week 8 vs MIN	1	8:28	1	10	MIN 11	3
Week 9 vs SF	1	13:49	1	10	GNB 41	6
Week 9 vs SF	2	11:39	2	10	SFO 38	11
Week 9 vs SF	2	7:56	2	7	SFO 11	2
Week 9 vs SF	3	11:08	1	10	SFO 28	4
Week 9 vs SF	3	8:07	2	9	SFO 9	8
Week 9 vs SF	4	11:01	1	10	SFO 43	-2
Week 10 vs JAX	2	4:29	1	10	JAX 30	4
Week 11 vs IND	2	9:11	2	2	CLT 21	4
Week 11 vs IND	4	8:52	1	10	GNB 23	9
Week 12 vs CHI	3	11:46	2	5	GNB 23	11
Week 15 vs CAR	1	3:04	1	10	GNB 45	6
Week 15 vs CAR	1	1:06	1	10	CAR 32	8
Week 15 vs CAR	2	5:20	2	7	CAR 21	8
Week 15 vs CAR	3	10:39	2	4	GNB 21	2
Week 15 vs CAR	4	6:44	1	10	GNB 46	3
Week 16 vs TEN	1	15:00	1	10	GNB 40	3
Week 16 vs TEN	2	12:09	2	4	OTI 14	1

Against odd front teams, the Packers liked to get into 21 personnel and run some old-fashioned Power. This was a big part of the game plan in week 15 vs Carolina's odd/tite package. The angles work well against these fronts. The tight end and PST can double team the defensive end, leaving the fullback to kick out a stand up outside linebacker. Additionally, the nose can be double teamed.

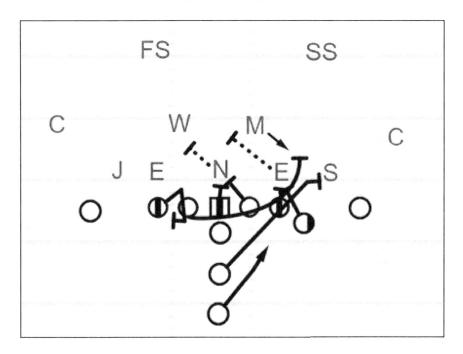

Against wide-9 even fronts, 1-back power is a nice concept to run. The tight end will base out on the wide-9 with an easy angle, creating a nice hole for the pulling guard.

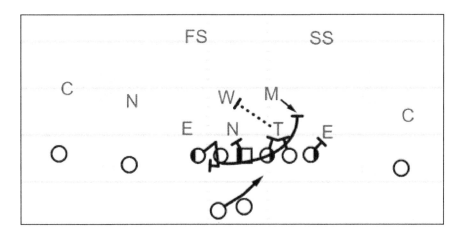

Even against a 6 technique 1-back power can be good if your tight end can handle the defensive end regardless.

Similar to inside zone and duo, the PSWR is responsible for a down safety on the front side of the run. The mechanics of that block are discussed in those sections.

In week 9, the Packers called their 2 TE 1-back power play, often with fake jet motion to the nub side. The 2-TE look is meant to get a double team on the play side defensive end. This idea holds for their base inside zone and duo schemes too.

Why it Worked: The Packers game planned this play nicely vs odd front teams,. Often getting the key double teams and movement at the point of attack.

Why it Didn't Work: In week 2, the play side linebacker filled hard, and the pulling guard pulled way to wide and didn't have his head up for the linebacker.

Jet Sweeps

Average Yards per Play	6.3

1st Down		3rd/4th Down (includes RZ)	
Called	Average	Called	Success Rate
3	1.7	0	0%
2nd Down 6-1		2nd Down 7+	
Called	Average	Called	Average
5	9.0	2	6.5
Red Zone 10-0		Red Zone 10-20	
Called	Touchdown %	Called	Touchdown %
0	0%	2	0%

Bear		Over		6-Man	
Called	Average	Called	Average	Called	Average
0	0.0	9	7.0	0	0.0
Under (4 Man)		**Mug**		**Under Sam Up**	
Called	Average	Called	Average	Called	Average
0	0.0	0	0.0	0	0.0
Wide		**Odd**		**Diamond**	
Called	Average	Called	Average	Called	Average
0	0.0	0	0.0	0	0.0

Week	Quarter	Time	Down	ToGo	Location	Yards
Week 1 vs MN	1	12:43	2	4	GNB 42	6
Week 1 vs MN	1	11:03	1	10	MIN 36	9
Week 1 vs MN	4	13:09	2	2	GNB 33	21
Week 1 vs MN	4	4:10	2	4	MIN 17	12
Week 7 vs HOU	3	8:15	2	4	GNB 31	-1
Week 8 vs MIN	3	8:17	1	10	MIN 37	0
Week 9 vs SF	4	10:20	2	12	SFO 45	9
Week 12 vs CHI	2	10:12	2	4	GNB 42	7
Week 13 vs PHI	4	12:54	1	10	PHI 26	-4
Week 17 vs CHI	2	6:27	2	8	CHI 20	4

This section covers "naked" jet sweeps, where the play side defensive end is left unblocked. This allows the offense to use the tight end for a second level block. Many defenses will have the defensive end read the tackle's block, so when the tackle works down the defensive end will squeeze down too. Defenses teach this technique to make the cutoff block for the tight end difficult on the back side of outside zone, as well as the base block on 1 back power.

The next diagram shows how the offense can get away with the end being unblocked against this technique.

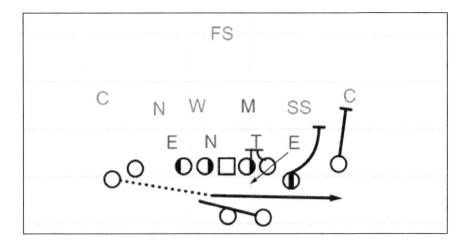

The PSWR will have the most dangerous man block. Against two high safeties that will rotate down late to the jet motion, he will block the strong safety leaving the corner unblocked. Against a pre-rotated single high defense, the PSWR will take the CB and the TE will have the strong safety. This is shown in the previous diagram.

Why it Worked: This concept had most of it's success in week 1 against Minnesota's 6 technique defensive ends that squeeze hard. This constraint play is able to gain a +1 block to the jet sweep.

Why it Didn't Work: In week 7 2nd & 4, the defensive end gets up field and does not squeeze the tackle. He is able to make the play in the backfield. This is also the case in the second week 13 clip.

Dragon

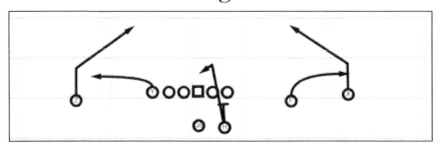

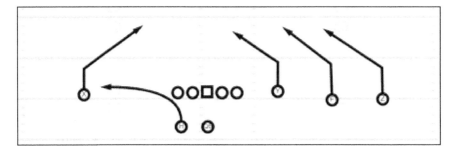

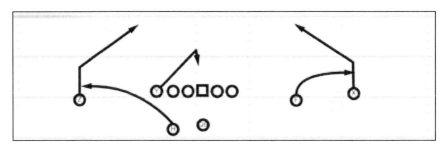

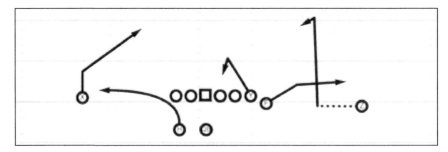

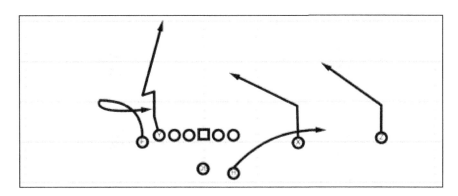

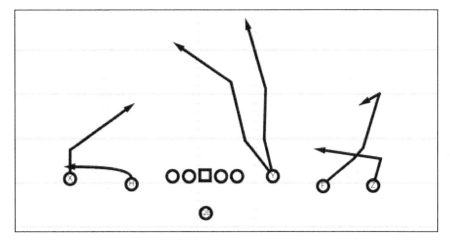

Average Yards per Play	5.1

1st Down		3rd/4th Down (includes RZ)	
Called	Average	Called	Success Rate
14	4.6	6	67%
2nd Down 6-1		**2nd Down 7+**	
Called	Average	Called	Average
4	5.0	9	4.4
Red Zone 10-0		**Red Zone 10-20**	
Called	Touchdown %	Called	Touchdown %
3	67%	4	0%

Cover 1		Cover 2		Cover 0	
Called	Average	Called	Average	Called	Average
7	6.9	8	6.8	1	0.0
Cover 3		**Cover 4**		**Cover 42**	
Called	Average	Called	Average	Called	Average
12	4.9	2	3.0	2	2.5
Cover 5		**Drop 8**		**5 Man Pressure**	
Called	Average	Called	Average	Called	Average
1	0.0	0	0	0	0

Week	Quarter	Time	Down	ToGo	Location	Yards
Week 1 vs MN	2	5:16	2	4	GNB 46	1
Week 1 vs MN	2	4:16	2	10	MIN 48	6
Week 2 vs DET	2	2:52	1	20	GNB 40	8
Week 3 vs NO	1	9:01	1	10	NOR 31	0
Week 3 vs NO	4	11:41	2	3	GNB 50	3
Week 4 vs ATL	2	3:19	1	10	ATL 15	-4
Week 4 vs ATL	2	1:31	2	5	ATL 45	9
Week 4 vs ATL	4	12:10	1	10	GNB 36	6
Week 4 vs ATL	4	10:06	2	7	ATL 49	5
Week 6 vs TB	2	0:59	2	10	GNB 25	9
Week 6 vs TB	3	9:11	2	23	GNB 11	5
Week 8 vs MIN	2	12:55	2	12	GNB 38	16
Week 8 vs MIN	2	9:00	1	10	MIN 17	0
Week 9 vs SF	1	15:00	1	10	GNB 25	5
Week 10 vs JAX	1	10:36	1	10	GNB 25	6
Week 10 vs JAX	3	12:10	1	10	GNB 2	22
Week 11 vs IND	3	6:59	2	7	GNB 17	3
Week 11 vs IND	3	0:24	3	1	GNB 31	0
Week 11 vs IND	4	4:01	2	9	CLT 42	1
Week 11 vs IND	4	1:25	1	10	GNB 6	0
Week 12 vs CHI	3	10:35	1	20	GNB 24	0
Week 13 vs PHI	1	7:08	2	16	GNB 19	-7
Week 13 vs PHI	2	13:46	1	10	PHI 48	12
Week 13 vs PHI	2	10:37	3	3	PHI 17	8
Week 13 vs PHI	2	1:05	3	4	PHI 25	25
Week 14 vs DET	1	4:24	3	4	GNB 47	5
Week 15 vs CAR	1	3:52	2	10	GNB 27	2
Week 16 vs TEN	1	1:52	2	4	GNB 46	7
Week 17 vs CHI	2	5:40	3	4	CHI 16	9
Week 17 vs CHI	4	3:50	1	4	CHI 4	4
Week 17 vs CHI	4	2:59	1	6	CHI 6	6
NFCCG vs TB	2	0:38	1	10	GNB 40	-7
NFCCG vs TB	3	0:26	3	2	TAM 2	2

Dragon has Long been a staple in Green Bay's offense, dating before LaFleur arrived. It always seemed Mike McCarthy's offenses ran Dragon more than anybody in football.

Aaron Rodgers must like the concept enough for the Packers to continue to run it as often as they do.

Rodgers' mastery of the concept can be seen with how he

manipulates his footwork with this concept. I have several tweets (@b_peters12) that show video examples of how well he runs the concept. Here are a few of them:

May 12 2020: One of the biggest benefits of post-snap defensive rotation is to bait QBs into bad looks in the 3-step game. This example shows Rodgers reading the post-snap safety rotation to hit one of the slant routes away from the rotation. He keeps his feet down the middle of the field until he recognizes the rotation, ensuring he will not be late to the slant.

April 23 2020: He initially sets his feet to work the Dragon concept to his left. When the corner traps the flat and the linebacker sits in the slant window, he gets the ball to the tight end on the over-the-ball route against cover 2. What makes this rep special is he doesn't even reset his feet to the over-the-ball route so he is still able to be on time and throw it before the tight end breaks. This isn't a long throw, most QB's can make this throw with enough practice. A critical element is the tight end running the route to the correct landmark, as he ends up right on the hash.

Why it Worked: Dragon is a call that Rodgers will often signal and check into vs certain looks. In week 13 on a 3rd and 3, Rodgers checks to Dragon on the weak side of an empty set (sixth diagram). The Eagles give a cover 1 look with the #2 defender playing from depth. Rodgers makes this check knowing he will throw the flat route with the man defender having to work over the top of the slant. The next image shows this play.

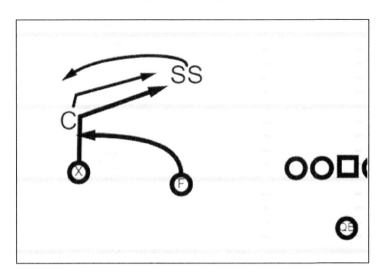

Why it Didn't Work: The first clip in week 1 shows the concept from 2x2 vs a Mike Zimmer staple overload fire zone blitz (while playing cover 4 behind it). Rodgers gets the ball out to the running back on the flat route, but Eric Kendricks does an awesome job of chasing the route down.

Omaha & Double Moves

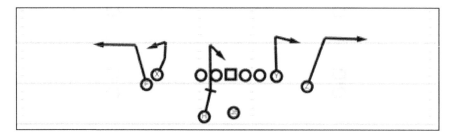

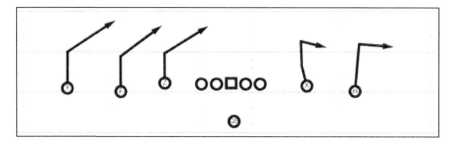

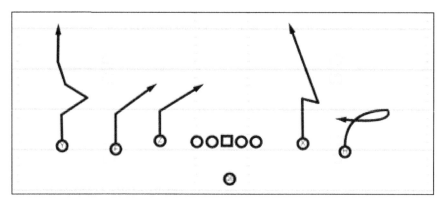

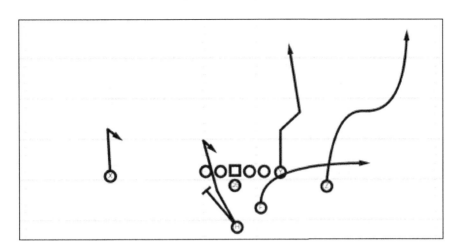

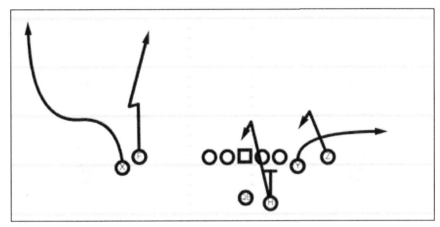

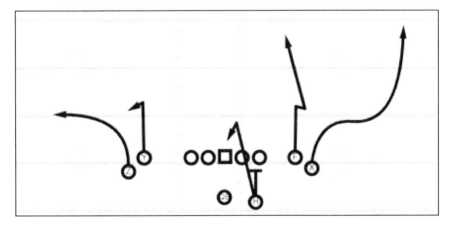

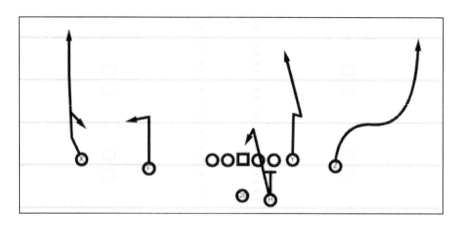

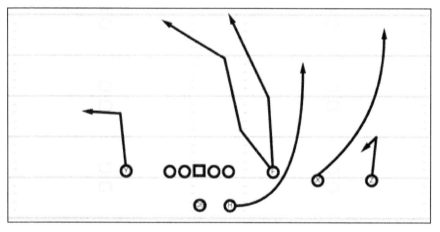

Average Yards per Play	8.0

1st Down		3rd/4th Down (includes RZ)	
Called	Average	Called	Success Rate
8	12.8	4	25%
2nd Down 6-1		2nd Down 7+	
Called	Average	Called	Average
3	6.3	6	7.8
Red Zone 10-0		Red Zone 10-20	
Called	Touchdown %	Called	Touchdown %
1	100%	1	0%

Cover 1		Cover 2		Cover 0	
Called	Average	Called	Average	Called	Average
6	8.7	2	12.5	1	0.0
Cover 3		**Cover 4**		**Cover 42**	
Called	Average	Called	Average	Called	Average
9	6.2	3	11.3	0	0
Cover 5		**Drop 8**		**5 Man Pressure**	
Called	Average	Called	Average	Called	Average
0	0	3	4.0	0	0

Week	Quarter	Time	Down	ToGo	Location	Yards
Week 1 vs MN	1	12:05	1	10	GNB 48	7
Week 1 vs MN	4	5:40	2	6	GNB 41	6
Week 2 vs DET	1	7:00	3	6	DET 42	0
Week 2 vs DET	1	5:52	3	3	DET 25	0
Week 2 vs DET	3	12:02	1	15	GNB 34	0
Week 2 vs DET	4	4:40	3	4	GNB 42	-6
Week 6 vs TB	1	5:24	1	10	TAM 41	0
Week 7 vs HOU	1	12:07	1	10	HTX 25	0
Week 8 vs MIN	1	11:41	2	1	MIN 38	5
Week 8 vs MIN	1	7:05	3	4	MIN 5	5
Week 9 vs SF	1	8:44	1	10	GNB 31	11
Week 9 vs SF	2	4:12	2	7	GNB 26	2
Week 14 vs DET	1	8:10	1	10	GNB 44	56
Week 14 vs DET	2	9:49	2	8	GNB 22	11
Week 14 vs DET	4	6:30	1	10	GNB 25	7
Week 15 vs CAR	2	3:22	2	10	GNB 25	12
Week 15 vs CAR	4	6:07	2	7	GNB 49	0
DIV vs LAR	1	12:48	2	8	GNB 34	8
DIV vs LAR	2	13:50	2	6	RAM 17	8
DIV vs LAR	2	0:29	1	10	GNB 25	21
NFCCG vs TB	1	10:25	2	7	GNB 28	14

Omaha is one of the most common terms used to describe a quick out cut from the #1 receiver within the structure of a 3-step concept. The out route is designed to take advantage of soft coverage from the corner.

The Packers paired the double move often. Rodgers hits

Lewis in the NFCCG on the nod route. Against cover 2 on this play, the Omaha side is covered, Rodgers resets nicely to the nod route.

Against press, the outside routes will convert to fades. The Packers hit one of the fade routes in week 14 for a touchdown to Adams.

The 8th diagram shows the Omaha route paired with the vertical concept. This gives the quarterback a quick answer vs pressure looks with the running back free releasing into the route.

Why it Worked: In general, this concept was very efficient for the Packers in 2020. Rodgers has been taking advantage of soft corners with this concept for years. It's a great way to get a simple completion to Adams as well. A good example of this is the 2nd play of the game vs LAR.

Why it Didn't Work: In week 2, the Lions played some catch-man on third downs and forced Rodgers to hold the ball and no throw the quick out cut. The DB's triggered hard on the quick out cuts. The catch-man technique does not convert to a fade as the receiver is not pressed at the line.

Slot Fade/Smash Split

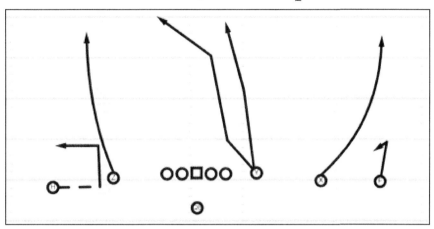

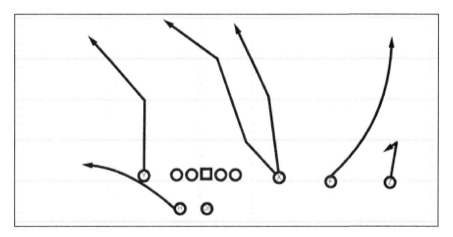

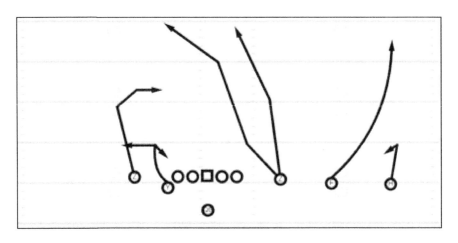

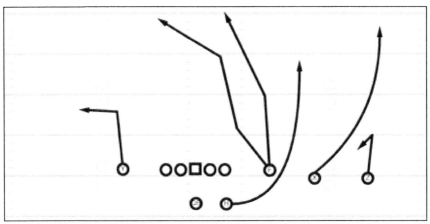

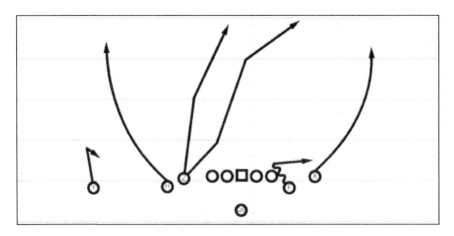

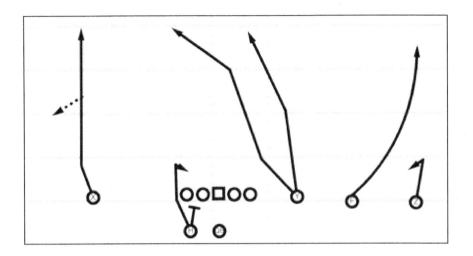

Average Yards per Play	11.6

1st Down		3rd/4th Down (includes RZ)	
Called	Average	Called	Success Rate
8	8.1	15	60%
2nd Down 6-1		2nd Down 7+	
Called	Average	Called	Average
1	7.0	12	8.1
Red Zone 10-0		Red Zone 10-20	
Called	Touchdown %	Called	Touchdown %
0	0%	2	0%

Week	Quarter	Time	Down	ToGo	Location	Yards
Week 2 vs DET	3	11:58	2	15	GNB 34	30
Week 2 vs DET	3	1:48	1	10	DET 17	0
Week 2 vs DET	4	11:01	3	4	GNB 32	41
Week 3 vs NO	1	8:57	2	10	NOR 31	-12
Week 4 vs ATL	1	6:03	3	7	ATL 25	19
Week 7 vs HOU	1	12:04	2	10	HTX 25	9
Week 7 vs HOU	3	3:10	2	10	GNB 24	0
Week 8 vs MIN	2	8:19	3	6	MIN 13	5
Week 8 vs MIN	4	0:47	1	10	GNB 28	7
Week 8 vs MIN	4	0:42	2	3	GNB 35	7
Week 9 vs SF	4	13:05	3	4	GNB 11	34
Week 9 vs SF	4	9:31	3	3	SFO 36	6
Week 11 vs IND	1	14:55	1	10	GNB 21	33
Week 11 vs IND	2	9:41	1	10	CLT 29	8
Week 11 vs IND	4	6:41	2	10	GNB 33	14
Week 11 vs IND	4	3:17	3	8	CLT 41	7
Week 11 vs IND	4	1:17	3	10	GNB 6	47
Week 11 vs IND	4	0:57	2	10	CLT 33	18
Week 12 vs CHI	2	11:38	3	2	GNB 28	8
Week 12 vs CHI	2	7:27	3	4	CHI 30	2
Week 12 vs CHI	3	10:32	2	20	GNB 24	0
Week 13 vs PHI	3	9:52	3	3	GNB 50	31
Week 13 vs PHI	3	1:59	2	10	GNB 37	5
Week 13 vs PHI	4	11:28	3	6	PHI 22	0
Week 14 vs DET	2	1:22	1	10	GNB 23	8
Week 14 vs DET	2	0:53	2	10	GNB 35	7
Week 14 vs DET	4	3:40	3	9	DET 34	0
Week 15 vs CAR	2	0:21	2	23	GNB 18	14
Week 16 vs TEN	2	13:30	1	10	OTI 34	0
Week 16 vs TEN	2	0:31	1	10	GNB 21	9
Week 16 vs TEN	4	4:01	3	10	OTI 41	32
Week 17 vs CHI	1	3:25	3	8	CHI 45	15
Week 17 vs CHI	4	9:04	2	7	GNB 40	0
DIV vs LAR	4	13:33	3	7	RAM 47	0
NFCCG vs TB	2	12:19	2	10	GNB 25	12
NFCCG vs TB	4	9:15	1	10	GNB 24	0

Cover 1		Cover 2		Cover 0	
Called	Average	Called	Average	Called	Average
11	15.5	11	11.4	2	16.0
Cover 3		Cover 4		Cover 42	
Called	Average	Called	Average	Called	Average
5	6.6	3	7.7	0	0
Cover 5		Drop 8		5 Man Pressure	
Called	Average	Called	Average	Called	Average
1	5.0	3	9.0	2	7.0

The Packers had quite a few big plays on the slot fade concept, typically to Davante Adams. When Adams is lined up as the #2 in trips, the slot fade is a top play call for Green Bay.

Slot fade is traditionally a concept saved for man coverage, and that is where the Packers made most of their big plays with the concept. The full field concept is usually called with zone beating routes and elements as well, making it an all purpose concept for LaFleur and staff.

The play is usually called from a three man surface. The #3 receiver will run a middle read route. He will run down the middle of the field vs two high and cross the safety's face to the opposite seam vs single high. The middle read route comes into play for the Packers more when they face a two high team, as the slot fade can be double-teamed. The next two diagrams show the middle read route adjusting to 1 high and two high coverage.

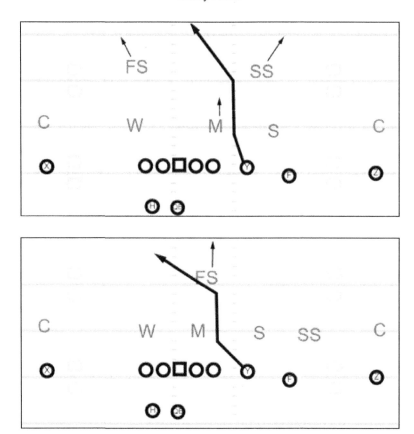

The Packers will also run it from a two man surface and mirror it as well out of empty.

When defenses play Cover 1 with a Robber/Rat, the man defenders will typically play with outside leverage. This makes the slot fade route harder to win. Davante Adams is a sensational route runner, so it is not as big of a problem for him to break that leverage. The Packers called this concept against all sorts of coverages, so this was not a common occurrence for them.

The first diagram shows a version used twice in week 9 vs San Francisco. The short motion to a stack is a nice way to get a free release for the low level control route and create a little more traffic for the slot fade defender. Against zone, this version makes the hi-low on the corner read easier for the quarterback as well. The corner has to get depth and width from a condensed set instead of just depth from normal splits.

The third diagram shows a variation used in week 8. The Packers have their drop-back bang dig concept called to the two man side, and it looks like Rodgers audibles to the slot fade on the three man side to get Adams on the slot fade route. With both concepts being front side concepts, Rodgers has to scramble when the slot fade side gets muddied.

The fourth diagram shows a variation that combines for verticals with he slot fade route. It even gets the RB on the seam. A nice marriage for two of the Packers favorite concepts. This version as called in week 7.

The fifth diagram shows a variation with bump protection.

Why it Worked: Aaron Rodgers' pinpoint accuracy against tight man coverage defined this concept for the Packers. Only a few quarterbacks in the NFL can consistently make the throws Rodgers made on this concept.

The first clip in the NFCCG shows the middle read route working open against man coverage (cover 1). MVS does a great job creating separation at the top of the route.

Rodgers hits MVS on the middle read route against cover 2 in week 11 at the end of the game on a critical 3rd & 10.

Why it Didn't Work: In week 3, the Saints bring a fifth rusher away from the center's slide in empty which brings a free rusher on Rodgers for a sack.

Lookie – Stick Nod

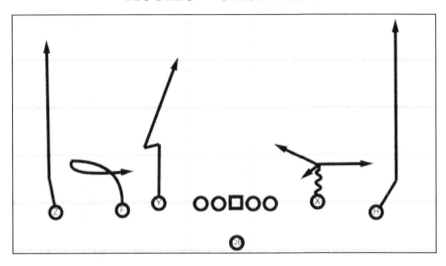

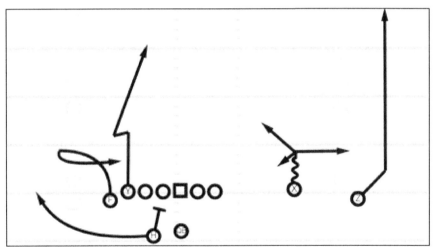

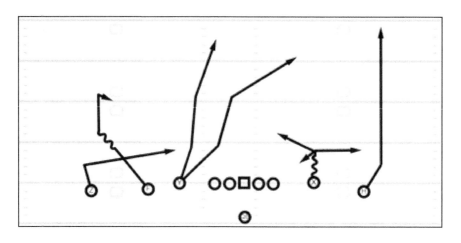

Average Yards per Play	6.2

1st Down		3rd/4th Down (includes RZ)	
Called	Average	Called	Success Rate
8	7.1	1	100%
2nd Down 6-1		**2nd Down 7+**	
Called	Average	Called	Average
2	7.0	7	4.3
Red Zone 10-0		**Red Zone 10-20**	
Called	Touchdown %	Called	Touchdown %
0	0%	5	0%

Cover 1		Cover 2		Cover 0	
Called	Average	Called	Average	Called	Average
4	5.5	4	6.3	1	12.0
Cover 3		**Cover 4**		**Cover 42**	
Called	Average	Called	Average	Called	Average
3	7.3	1	7.0	0	0
Cover 5		**Drop 8**		**5 Man Pressure**	
Called	Average	Called	Average	Called	Average
3	5.0	3	11.0	2	4.0

Week	Quarter	Time	Down	ToGo	Location	Yards
Week 1 vs MN	2	8:23	2	10	MIN 12	0
Week 2 vs DET	2	0:22	1	10	DET 11	0
Week 6 vs TB	2	1:02	1	10	GNB 25	0
Week 11 vs IND	2	1:52	1	10	GNB 25	5
Week 11 vs IND	4	4:45	1	20	GNB 47	11
Week 12 vs CHI	1	7:34	2	10	CHI 12	0
Week 12 vs CHI	1	5:14	1	10	GNB 25	8
Week 12 vs CHI	1	3:55	1	10	GNB 36	15
Week 13 vs PHI	4	12:11	2	14	PHI 30	8
Week 14 vs DET	1	0:13	1	10	DET 27	12
Week 16 vs TEN	1	14:23	2	7	GNB 43	7
Week 16 vs TEN	1	10:42	2	5	OTI 12	7
Week 16 vs TEN	1	1:52	2	4	GNB 46	7
Week 16 vs TEN	3	6:20	2	8	OTI 47	8
Week 17 vs CHI	4	11:22	1	10	GNB 24	6
DIV vs LAR	2	14:36	2	7	RAM 36	0
NFCCG vs TB	3	12:31	3	3	GNB 32	10
NFCCG vs TB	3	1:39	2	9	TAM 12	7

Davante Adams made a killing on the Lookie route in 2020. The Lookie route is a version of the weak side option out of a two man spread alignment. Often the term "slant 'till you can't" applies to this route. The offense wants the Lookie route to win inside because that's where the big plays usually come from. This will happen most often against single high man and aggressive match coverage.

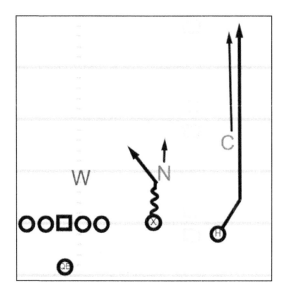

If the #2 defender plays with hard inside leverage, typically in a two high shell, the Lookie will break out.

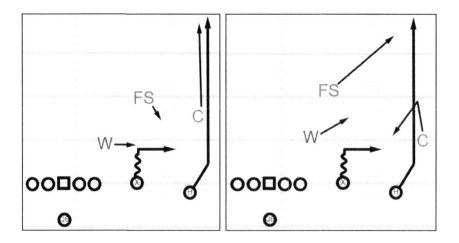

Against soft cover three, the Lookie route will settle down in the void between the hook and flat defender.

The back side stick nod comes into play when the defense gets three over two on the Lookie side. Against two high, the Mike is isolated on the nod, with the return route coming under as a check down.

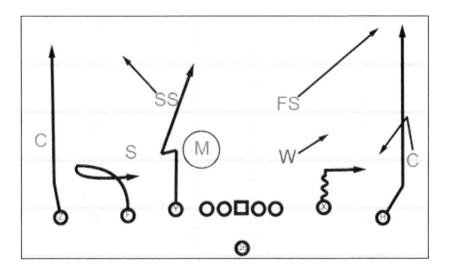

Against single high, the strong hook player is isolated on the nod. The return route will be working with inside leverage against single high as well, so the return route becomes more of an option in this case. The nod route will stay wider to avoid the high safety as well and to further define the stretch on the strong hook player.

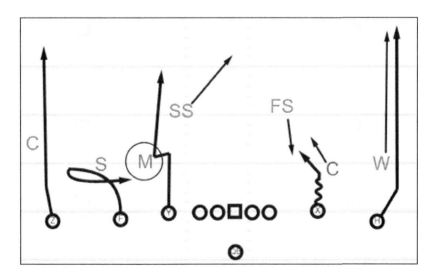

Why it Worked: Week 11 shows two good contrasting clips for the Lookie route working 1 on 1 vs two high. Adams breaks out on the first one, and breaks in on the second one.

In the second week 12 clip, Rodgers gets to the return route against Chicago's drop-8 coverage.

The other two week 12 clips show Adams working the Lookie route against man coverage, although he slips on one of them.

Why it Didn't Work: In week 6, the Bucs bring a simulated pressure and play cover 2 trap behind it. Rodgers throws the Lookie route hot, settling in the void vacated by the "blitzer". Adams drifts slightly and the ball from Rodgers is slightly off with the corner trap and dropping linebacker fast approaching.

Mesh

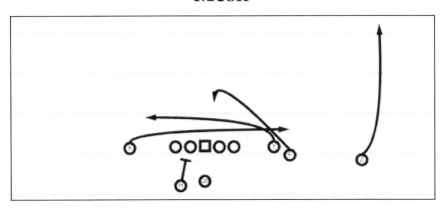

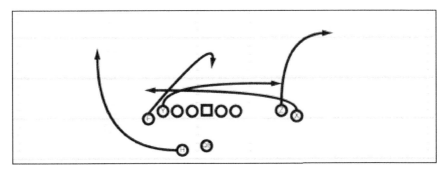

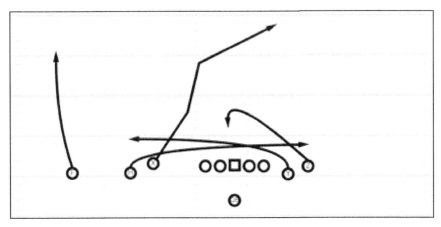

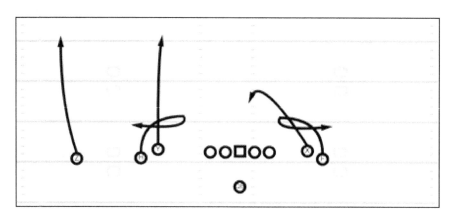

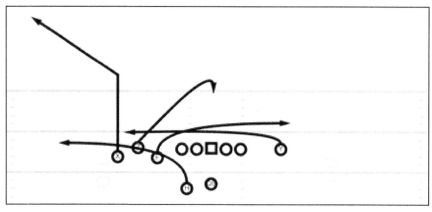

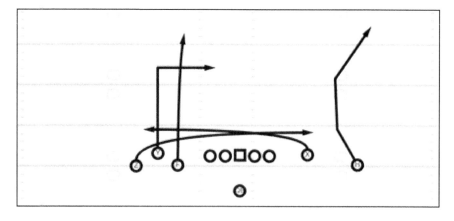

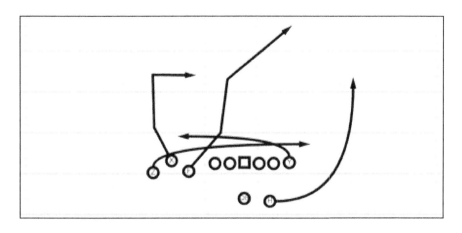

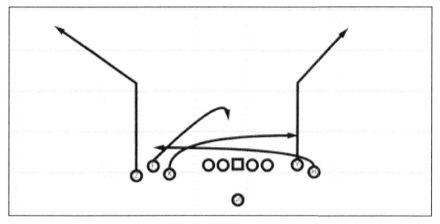

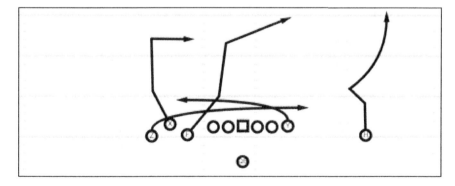

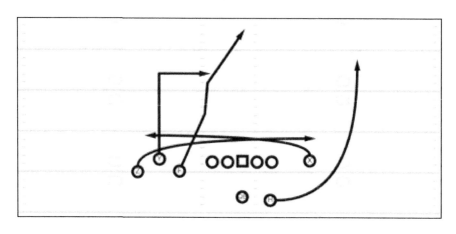

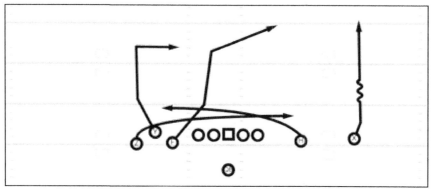

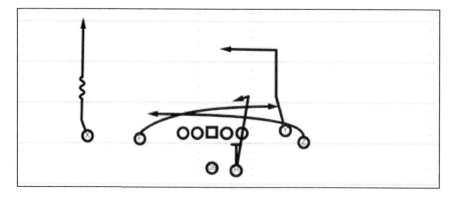

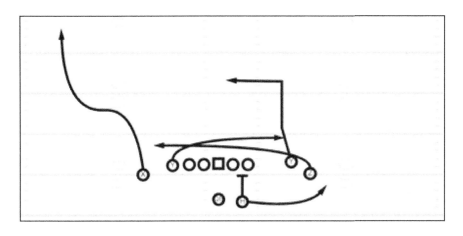

Average Yards per Play	8.4

1st Down		3rd/4th Down (includes RZ)	
Called	Average	Called	Success Rate
5	5.8	21	57%
2nd Down 6-1		**2nd Down 7+**	
Called	Average	Called	Average
5	11.4	3	7.7
Red Zone 10-0		**Red Zone 10-20**	
Called	Touchdown %	Called	Touchdown %
4	50%	4	25%

Cover 1		Cover 2		Cover 0	
Called	Average	Called	Average	Called	Average
14	8.3	1	49.0	4	1.8
Cover 3		**Cover 4**		**Cover 42**	
Called	Average	Called	Average	Called	Average
6	7.8	1	0.0	0	0
Cover 5		**Drop 8**		**5 Man Pressure**	
Called	Average	Called	Average	Called	Average
2	-5.0	1	-2.0	7	10.3

Week	Quarter	Time	Down	ToGo	Location	Yards
Week 1 vs MN	1	1:58	2	5	GNB 44	0
Week 1 vs MN	2	10:38	2	5	MIN 46	18
Week 1 vs MN	4	10:52	1	5	MIN 5	1
Week 2 vs DET	2	14:10	2	5	GNB 39	22
Week 2 vs DET	2	13:05	1	10	DET 28	4
Week 2 vs DET	2	10:13	3	3	DET 7	7
Week 2 vs DET	3	5:25	3	2	GNB 33	25
Week 2 vs DET	3	3:27	1	10	DET 30	4
Week 2 vs DET	3	1:40	3	10	DET 17	0
Week 2 vs DET	4	8:41	3	6	DET 23	9
Week 4 vs ATL	3	5:24	3	3	ATL 21	21
Week 6 vs TB	1	12:10	1	10	TAM 35	12
Week 7 vs HOU	1	12:34	2	5	GNB 43	17
Week 7 vs HOU	1	11:31	3	1	HTX 16	8
Week 7 vs HOU	2	7:29	3	2	HTX 44	0
Week 7 vs HOU	4	4:41	3	7	HTX 30	16
Week 9 vs SF	2	15:00	3	4	GNB 31	0
Week 9 vs SF	2	9:41	3	8	SFO 25	7
Week 9 vs SF	3	11:47	3	7	GNB 23	49
Week 10 vs JAX	1	13:39	3	3	GNB 32	0
Week 10 vs JAX	3	7:15	4	3	JAX 33	0
Week 10 vs JAX	3	1:21	3	8	JAX 47	TO
Week 12 vs CHI	2	6:40	4	2	CHI 28	14
Week 14 vs DET	2	14:18	2	9	DET 14	14
Week 14 vs DET	3	14:56	2	10	GNB 25	3
Week 14 vs DET	3	8:25	2	10	DET 21	6
Week 14 vs DET	3	7:42	3	4	DET 15	5
Week 14 vs DET	3	2:42	3	3	GNB 43	11
Week 15 vs CAR	3	9:58	3	2	GNB 23	-9
Week 15 vs CAR	3	3:22	3	4	GNB 46	-2
DIV vs LAR	1	8:52	2	5	RAM 5	0
NFCCG vs TB	2	1:14	3	6	GNB 17	23
NFCCG vs TB	3	14:10	3	5	GNB 30	-1
NFCCG vs TB	3	9:33	1	8	TAM 8	8
NFCCG vs TB	3	2:59	3	2	TAM 24	11
NFCCG vs TB	4	11:32	3	5	GNB 24	-10

The Packers are the best "Mesh" team in the NFL. They run more variations than any other team I have studied.

The Mesh concept is identified by the two shallow crossing routes intersecting over the ball at about 3 yards. Offensive coaches at all levels will get to this concept in some form or fashion, and everybody has different rules for how the routes are taught and their framework within the overall concept.

The Packers check into Mesh vs optimal looks (man coverage) and check out of it vs bad looks (zone/match). Coverage indicators help Rodgers correctly identify to check in/out of it, RB's lined up wide and various motions.

Mesh is a featured part of the Packers game plans vs the Lions, who often play man coverage.

The Mesh concept is a hot topic amongst offensive coaching circles. Either you love it or hate it. If designed properly, mesh can be an all-purpose concept in an offensive system. In general, the Packers have created a structure around the concept to give it a lasting impact for them week to week. Here are a few of my mesh check points that can make it an all purpose concept.

- Quick first read for the quarterback to combat blitzes and quick pressure.
- Zone answer early in the progression
- Treat the mesh as the last part of the progression.

The Packers take this one step further and often call a double move as the first read, then work the mesh later in the progression.

Often times the Packers would call it with a quick tempo in order to create confusion on man coverage assignments. This worked for a touchdown in week 2.

The variation shown in the 4th diagram gets "four strong" for the offense. Releasing the running back to the trips/bunch side creates extra confusion for the defense. In week 9, the Packers paired this version with tempo while aligning Davante Adams in the backfield. Aligning Adams in the backfield creates further man coverage matchup confusion.

Why it Worked: The big play in week 9 the Packers hit Adams on an outside stutter-go route. The 49ers play with a two high shell, but the safety stays low and inside, which leaves Adams in a 1 on 1.

Why it Didn't Work: Tampa Bay had a strong game plan for Mesh on third downs in the NFCCG. Bowles played man under with two deep, but the two deep defenders were disguised and ended up robbing underneath and cutting any in-breaking routes. The next image shows the defense in action on the Aaron Jones fumble.

The man defenders play with outside leverage because of the robbing safeties. The Will linebacker has no chance of making it through the mess in the middle of the field, so having the Strong Safety as a cutter/robber is a great strategy against the Packers running mesh against man under looks.

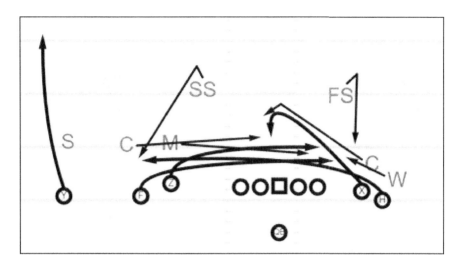

Shallow

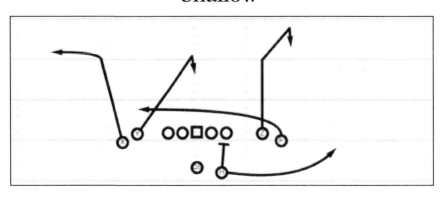

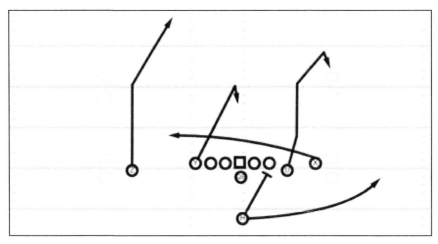

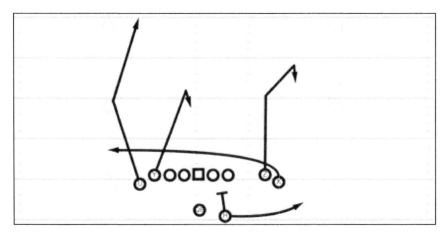

Average Yards per Play	8.3

1st Down		3rd/4th Down (includes RZ)	
Called	Average	Called	Success Rate
1	0.0	3	33%
2nd Down 6-1		2nd Down 7+	
Called	Average	Called	Average
2	12.5	4	12.3
Red Zone 10-0		Red Zone 10-20	
Called	Touchdown %	Called	Touchdown %
0	0%	1	0%

Cover 1		Cover 2		Cover 0	
Called	Average	Called	Average	Called	Average
2	5.0	0	0.0	1	9.0
Cover 3		Cover 4		Cover 42	
Called	Average	Called	Average	Called	Average
5	8.0	2	8.0	0	0.0
Cover 5		Drop 8		5 Man Pressure	
Called	Average	Called	Average	Called	Average
0	0.0	0	0.0	0	0.0

Week	Quarter	Time	Down	ToGo	Location	Yards
Week 6 vs TB	2	12:50	3	10	GNB 22	TO
Week 7 vs HOU	1	2:32	2	8	GNB 14	8
Week 7 vs HOU	3	7:29	3	5	GNB 30	9
Week 10 vs JAX	2	3:50	2	6	JAX 26	18
Week 10 vs JAX	2	1:28	1	10	JAX 26	0
Week 12 vs CHI	1	0:47	2	8	CHI 16	11
Week 15 vs CAR	4	3:51	3	6	CAR 25	-8
Week 17 vs CHI	4	10:37	2	4	GNB 30	7
DIV vs LAR	2	8:50	2	9	RAM 46	14
NFCCG vs TB	3	10:23	2	10	TAM 24	16

The Shallow concept is a pure progression read in most systems. The progression works as follows:

1. Shallow
2. Middle Sit
3. Curl/Swirl
4. Check Down

The design of the play is to create separation with the shallow route against man coverage, and space out zone defenders with the middle sit and curl/swirl.

Why it Worked: The Packers get a completion off a scramble drill with a busted route in the NFCCG.

When the concept worked for the Packers, it was most often Adams coming open on the Shallow route. This was the case in both week 7 clips and the completion in week 10.

Against the Rams, Rodgers gets to his check down. This clip is good teach tape for QB coaches to show the value of the check down.

Why it Didn't Work: The Bucs get a pick six in week 6. Rodgers throws Adams on the comeback to the boundary, but the corner triggers hard on a ball left slightly inside.

This concept does not have a true front side/quick blitz answer. If the shallow and middle sit are covered, there isn't often enough time left in the pocket to get to the curl/swirl or check down. Additionally, many zone and match coverages can pass off and bracket the concept.

Middle Read

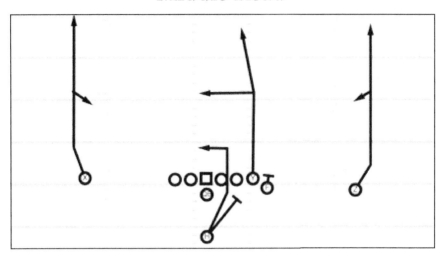

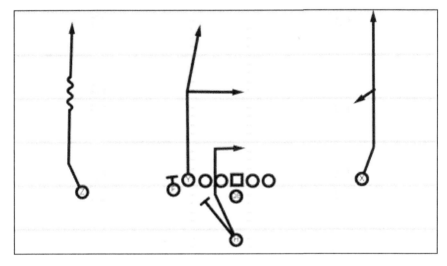

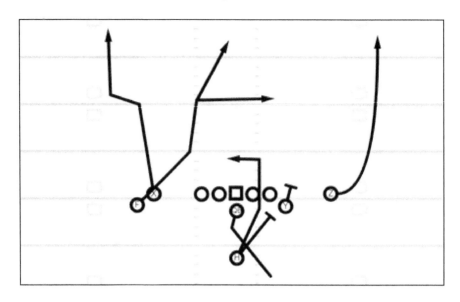

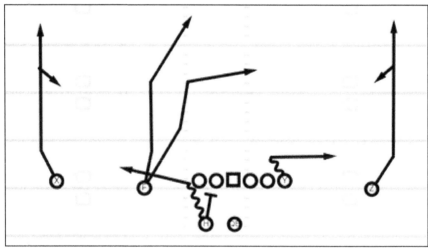

140

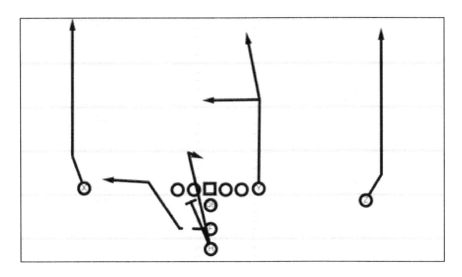

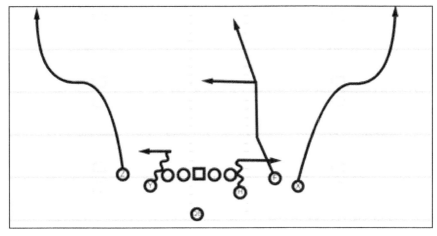

Average Yards per Play	16.8

1st Down		3rd/4th Down (includes RZ)	
Called	Average	Called	Success Rate
6	18.8	4	50%
2nd Down 6-1		**2nd Down 7+**	
Called	Average	Called	Average
0	0.0	2	20.0
Red Zone 10-0		**Red Zone 10-20**	
Called	Touchdown %	Called	Touchdown %
0	0%	0	0%

Cover 1		Cover 2		Cover 0	
Called	Average	Called	Average	Called	Average
1	78.0	1	0.0	1	28.0
Cover 3		**Cover 4**		**Cover 42**	
Called	Average	Called	Average	Called	Average
7	13.7	0	0	0	0
Cover 5		**Drop 8**		**5 Man Pressure**	
Called	Average	Called	Average	Called	Average
1	0.0	0	0	1	0.0

Week	Quarter	Time	Down	ToGo	Location	Yards
Week 2 vs DET	2	6:07	1	10	GNB 10	8
Week 7 vs HOU	1	0:50	3	9	GNB 23	28
Week 9 vs SF	1	11:48	2	8	SFO 36	36
Week 10 vs JAX	2	15:00	1	10	GNB 22	78
Week 10 vs JAX	3	9:24	1	10	GNB 43	0
Week 12 vs CHI	4	9:00	3	13	GNB 40	0
Week 14 vs DET	2	7:09	2	9	GNB 44	4
Week 14 vs DET	3	9:33	3	14	DET 42	21
Week 14 vs DET	3	4:50	1	10	GNB 21	15
Week 17 vs CHI	3	12:33	3	13	GNB 44	0
DIV vs LAR	1	10:56	1	10	RAM 46	12
DIV vs LAR	3	10:09	1	17	GNB 8	0

The Middle Read concept consists of a slot receiver or tight end running the middle read route, and outside receivers on isolation-type routes.

The middle read route is a critical component of a few of the Packers concepts in their pass game. The route will work deep over the middle of the field vs two high safeties and cross the free safety's face vs single high. The next two diagrams show the route drawn out against both looks.

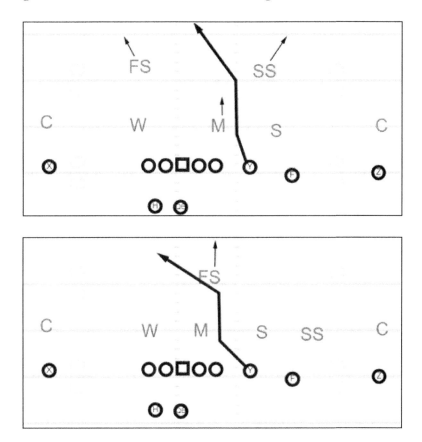

The Packers appeared to run two different versions of the concept.

Against single high coverage, the Packers focused on

working the isolation routes on the outside. Without safety help, Adams would typically get 1 on 1 matchups with this concept. Based on the leverage of the corner defending him, the Packers could run a fade, comeback, or hinge route with an outside release. The next diagram shows how Adams, lined up as the X receiver, gets a 1 on 1 with the corner. If the defense gets safety help or the Will linebacker gets underneath a hinge or comeback, Rodgers can work the middle read or check downs

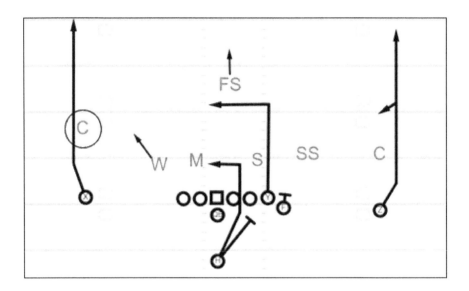

Why it Worked: In weeks 9 and 10, Rodgers hits the outside fade routes for big plays.

In week 7, Houston brings a zero blitz and Rodgers is still able to hit Adams on the outside fade route.

Why it Didn't Work: Two high coverage gave this concept problems on the couple of snaps the Packers ran it against. The defense is able to get a bracket on Adams and force Rodgers to look inside on the middle read route and check downs.

Middle Read – Dagger

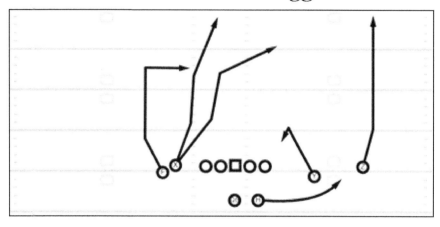

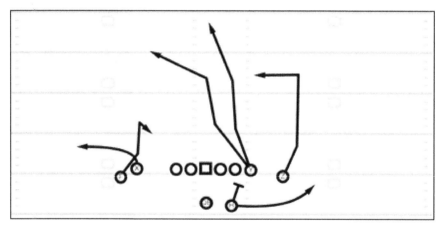

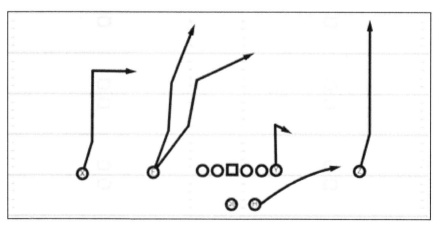

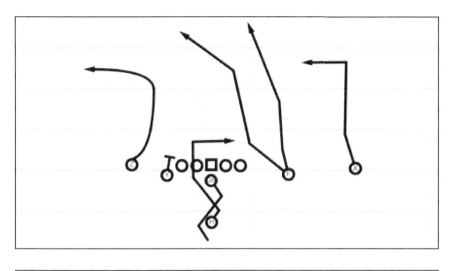

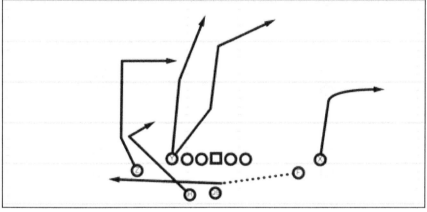

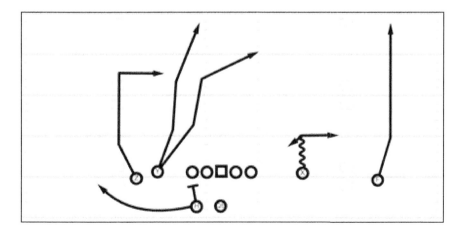

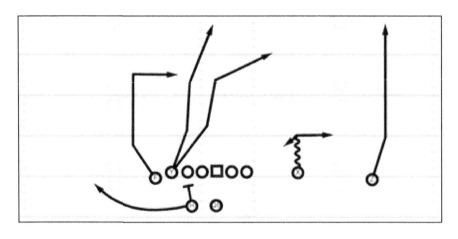

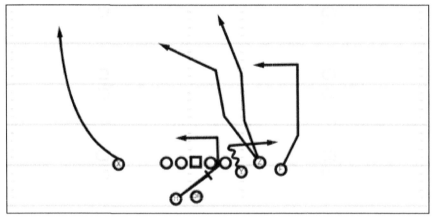

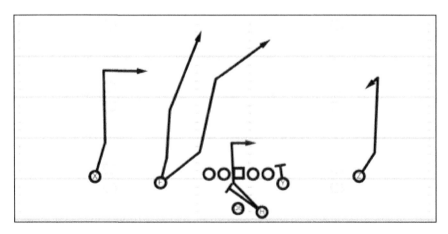

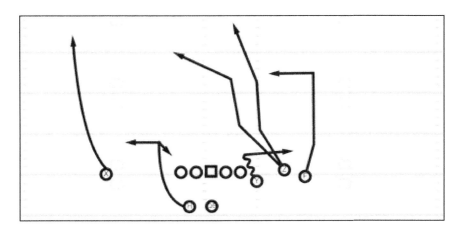

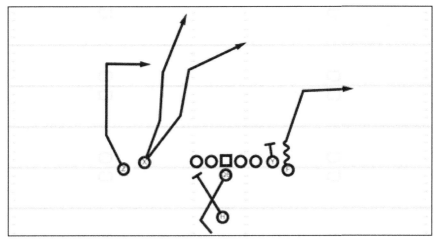

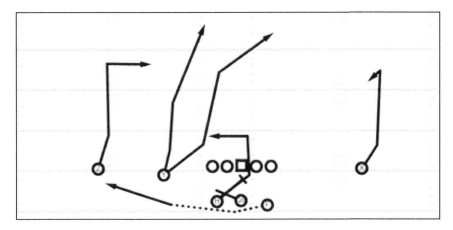

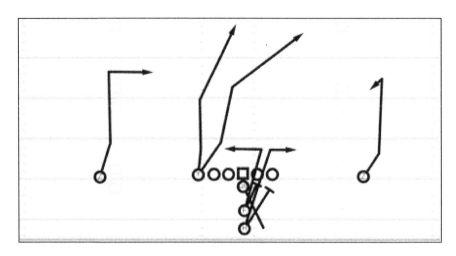

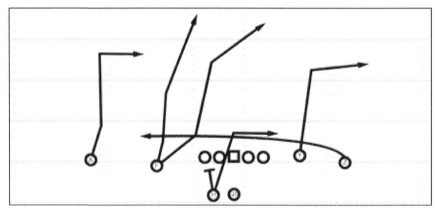

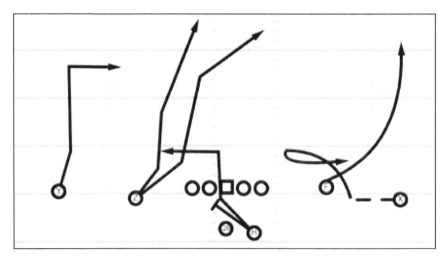

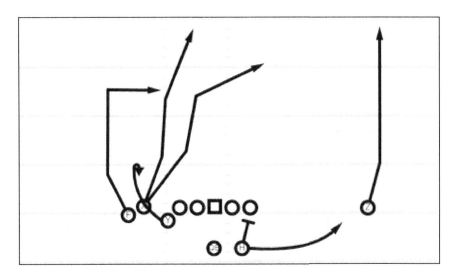

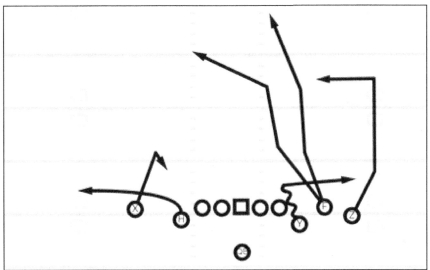

Average Yards per Play	5.7

1st Down		3rd/4th Down (includes RZ)	
Called	Average	Called	Success Rate
17	6.4	13	38%
2nd Down 6-1		**2nd Down 7+**	
Called	Average	Called	Average
4	10.3	12	4.1
Red Zone 10-0		**Red Zone 10-20**	
Called	Touchdown %	Called	Touchdown %
0	0%	1	0%

Cover 1		Cover 2		Cover 0	
Called	Average	Called	Average	Called	Average
12	5.1	9	6.8	0	0
Cover 3		**Cover 4**		**Cover 42**	
Called	Average	Called	Average	Called	Average
18	4.2	0	0	2	12.0
Cover 5		**Drop 8**		**5 Man Pressure**	
Called	Average	Called	Average	Called	Average
2	0.0	0	0	3	14.0

Week	Quarter	Time	Down	ToGo	Location	Yards
Week 1 vs MN	3	11:57	1	10	GNB 9	8
Week 1 vs MN	4	11:50	2	7	MIN 43	0
Week 3 vs NO	1	1:18	3	12	NOR 33	13
Week 4 vs ATL	1	13:33	1	10	GNB 27	0
Week 4 vs ATL	2	7:38	1	10	GNB 25	17
Week 4 vs ATL	2	5:18	3	10	ATL 47	14
Week 4 vs ATL	3	7:12	1	10	GNB 49	23
Week 4 vs ATL	4	7:24	2	13	ATL 31	-12
Week 6 vs TB	1	13:30	1	10	GNB 45	8
Week 6 vs TB	2	0:21	2	10	GNB 39	-12
Week 6 vs TB	3	10:13	1	10	GNB 24	-8
Week 6 vs TB	3	5:40	3	8	GNB 47	0
Week 7 vs HOU	1	1:19	2	10	GNB 22	1
Week 8 vs MIN	3	8:12	3	10	MIN 37	0
Week 8 vs MIN	3	8:07	4	10	MIN 37	0
Week 8 vs MIN	4	4:24	2	5	GNB 43	2
Week 9 vs SF	1	7:12	3	5	GNB 47	0
Week 9 vs SF	1	0:11	2	8	GNB 27	4
Week 10 vs JAX	1	0:20	3	3	GNB 16	6
Week 10 vs JAX	2	6:24	1	10	JAX 40	3
Week 11 vs IND	2	14:09	1	10	GNB 40	20
Week 11 vs IND	2	13:24	1	10	CLT 40	5
Week 11 vs IND	3	6:16	3	4	GNB 20	0
Week 11 vs IND	4	5:54	1	10	GNB 47	10
Week 12 vs CHI	1	14:22	1	10	GNB 36	0
Week 12 vs CHI	2	12:17	2	10	GNB 20	8
Week 13 vs PHI	2	14:22	2	5	GNB 42	10
Week 13 vs PHI	2	13:08	1	10	PHI 36	9
Week 13 vs PHI	3	2:55	1	10	GNB 24	0
Week 13 vs PHI	3	2:50	2	10	GNB 24	13
Week 13 vs PHI	3	1:15	3	5	GNB 42	11
Week 14 vs DET	1	8:51	2	6	GNB 29	15
Week 14 vs DET	1	5:03	2	7	GNB 44	3
Week 14 vs DET	2	0:50	3	3	GNB 42	1
Week 14 vs DET	3	12:56	2	6	GNB 37	14
Week 14 vs DET	3	11:06	1	20	DET 48	-1
Week 15 vs CAR	1	4:31	3	7	GNB 28	14
Week 15 vs CAR	2	1:50	3	20	GNB 49	10
Week 15 vs CAR	3	14:23	3	7	GNB 28	0
Week 15 vs CAR	4	8:39	1	10	GNB 25	10
Week 16 vs TEN	4	13:19	2	16	GNB 47	5
Week 17 vs CHI	1	6:47	2	11	GNB 19	15
Week 17 vs CHI	1	4:03	2	11	CHI 48	3
DIV vs LAR	3	14:20	1	10	RAM 15	0
DIV vs LAR	3	10:03	2	17	GNB 8	21
NFCCG vs TB	2	10:20	1	10	TAM 47	5
NFCCG vs TB	4	8:26	3	10	GNB 24	0

The Middle Read – Dagger is an all-purpose drop back and play action concept in the Packers offense. The ability to attack any coverage and adjust the protection using bump-flats, max protection, or 6 man protection gives the play caller endless ways to adjust the concept each week.

When used in the drop back game, Middle Read-Dagger is most commonly paired with the underneath weak option. These versions can be seen in the 6th and 7th diagrams. With the middle read and dagger working into the quarterback's vision, the ability for the weak option runner to break inside is taken away to not muddy the picture on the back side. Against most looks, he will run the speed out. Against softer cover 3 with an outside leveraged flat player, he will sit down.

Davante Adams is most often running the weak option as the X receiver for the Packers each week. Getting Adams the first read in the progression on this play is a great way to get him more touches in the game. Also, he excels at winning on the out cut against outside leverage man. A great example of this can be seen in week 10 vs JAX.

Similar to the weak option, the Packers like to work the Stick/Spot concept (two man and three man) on the front side. This quick hitting concept has potential to get the ball into Jones or Williams hands in the flat quickly while horizontally stretching the flat defender. If the defense does a good job of expanding for the Stick/Spot, the Middle read will work to replace the vertical space behind the defenders. The next diagram shows the spacing created on the back side against single high. The middle read replaces the vertical space left open with the front side hook and flat defenders clamping down on the Stick/Spot. This route opens up more against spot-drop cover 3 schemes.

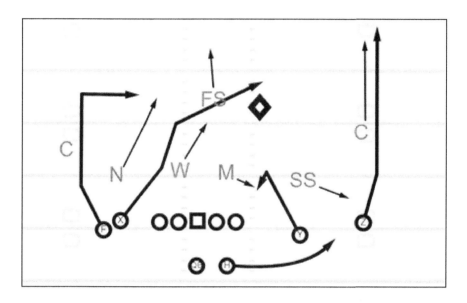

If the nickel and ILB wall/bracket the middle read, the dagger route will have inside leverage on the corner. Most often against single high (man or zone match), the nickel/#2 defender will carry the middle read and open up space for the dagger. A great example of this is week 4 2Q 7:38.

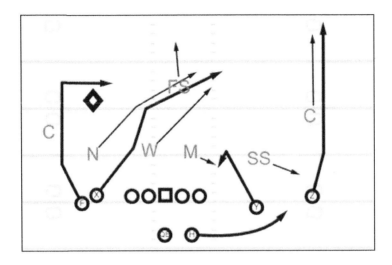

Against two high, the Stick/Snag will have a better chance of getting horizontal space for the front side. In week 4, the Packers hit the outside vertical in the "Turkey Hole" of Atlanta's Tampa 2 coverage. In week 11, the Packers called the two man stick version against Indy's Tampa 2. Rodgers works to the RB check-swing as the last read in his progression on this version.

The Packers also worked two man Stick/Snag front side, without the vertical. With these (as well as the weak option) called, the back would most often check release to the side of the Dagger. This version provides a hi-low on the Dagger concept. The next image shows how the flat defender is placed in the hi-low against a cover 4 defense.

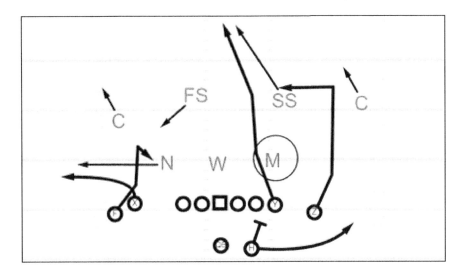

Another common front side route is the Hinge route. This can be seen in the 9th , 12th, and 13th diagrams. This route is a way to isolate Adams or another outside receiver while getting another body in protection or to bump before check-releasing.

The middle read and dagger routes act as the back side of the progression. This concept is very similar to the Air Raid Y Cross concept. It reads out the same and attacks similar land marks. The biggest benefit of the middle read route is the ability for the slot receiver to occupy the near safety against cover 4. This will isolate the dig route on the corner without the threat of a safety robbing.

The fifth diagram shows how the Packers incorporate the concept within their fake jet RB free release package. A Nice compliment for the four vertical concept often used off this action.

In week 13, the Packers called the variation shown in the next diagram against the Eagles wide-9 over front on three occasions. With the strong safety having to fit the C-gap, the response to the flat off play action is slower. This leaves the corner on an island with he quick comeback route. If the strong safety had the D gap, he could play his run/pass responsibilities easier. This is a great example of a game plan putting a specific defender in extreme conflict based on his responsibilities.

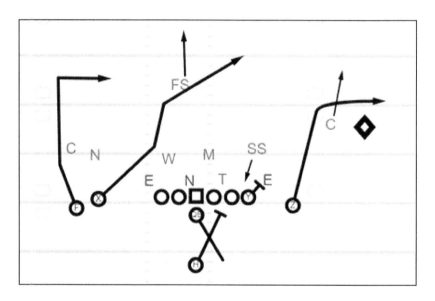

The 15th diagram shows a version called on 3rd down in week 15. The front side concept with Adams running the whip route with short motion is a nice quick man beater. Against zone coverage when the whip can be passed back and forth with three defenders over two, the QB can work the Middle Read to Dagger routes.

Why it Worked: The Packers understanding of this concept makes it effective for them in both the drop back game and off play action. Pairing quick game concepts or isolation routes on the front side give the quarterback a strong first option.

The 3rd 12 conversion in week 3 was called against a man coverage scheme and Rodgers took off and ran for the first down.

On the week 4 third down conversion, Rodgers hits the isolated hinge route against a neat five man pressure from the Falcons. Out of a bear look, the drop both edge players and bring a backer and a safety up the middle. Even with the pressure bearing down, Rodgers is able to get the ball out at the top of his drop without getting hit. Elite quarterbacks have multiple ways of avoiding pressure, and in this case Rodgers uses his first-read timing to avoid a sack.

Why it Didn't Work: The Bucs bring edge pressure in week 6 when the Packers called the concept off play action. The running back was not able to pick up the blitz in time and Rodgers gets sacked.

In week 9, Rodgers tries the isolated fade route to Adams on a third down. The Pass is broken up by the corner. Great technique from the corner in this clip.

Middle Read – Drive (Shadow)

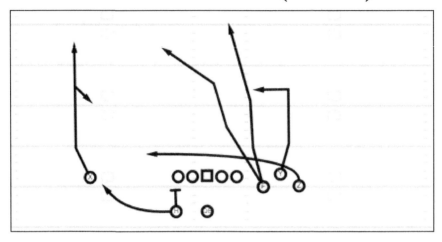

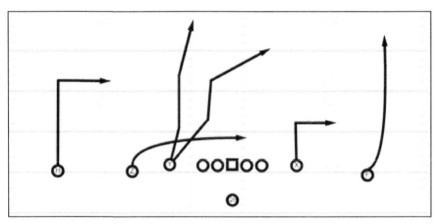

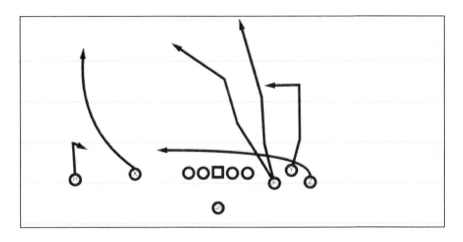

Average Yards per Play	7.1

1st Down		3rd/4th Down (includes RZ)	
Called	Average	Called	Success Rate
0	0.0	7	57%
2nd Down 6-1		**2nd Down 7+**	
Called	Average	Called	Average
1	10.0	0	0.0
Red Zone 10-0		**Red Zone 10-20**	
Called	Touchdown %	Called	Touchdown %
0	0%	0	0%

Cover 1		Cover 2		Cover 0	
Called	Average	Called	Average	Called	Average
1	0.0	0	0	0	0
Cover 3		**Cover 4**		**Cover 42**	
Called	Average	Called	Average	Called	Average
0	0.0	0	0	1	12.0
Cover 5		**Drop 8**		**5 Man Pressure**	
Called	Average	Called	Average	Called	Average
2	7.5	0	0	4	7.5

Week	Quarter	Time	Down	ToGo	Location	Yards
Week 1 vs MN	3	7:39	3	6	GNB 41	0
Week 2 vs DET	1	8:26	3	8	GNB 39	15
Week 2 vs DET	2	12:20	2	6	DET 24	10
Week 10 vs JAX	2	7:04	3	7	GNB 48	12
Week 10 vs JAX	3	7:21	3	3	JAX 33	0
Week 12 vs CHI	1	12:19	3	7	CHI 47	8
Week 12 vs CHI	1	1:47	3	4	CHI 28	10
Week 12 vs CHI	2	7:27	3	4	CHI 30	2

Middle Read – Drive reads out as a pure progression. QB should work the ISO receiver/Fade-Flat/Slot Fade first, then the middle read and drive working into his vision.

Against true man coverage, the drive route defender must get through four bodies to stick with his receiver. A tough task for the stingiest of corners.

Many teams will check to a zone or match coverage against the three man bunch to prevent this exact scenario for the man defender. In this case, the inside release of the middle read and the drive will ensure this first inside defender is in a high-low. If he stays low on the drive route, the middle read route should open up. The next two diagrams show the defender placed in a hi-low vs 1 high and 2 high.

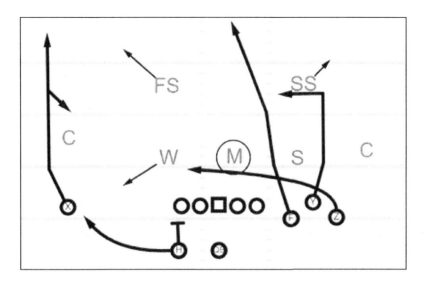

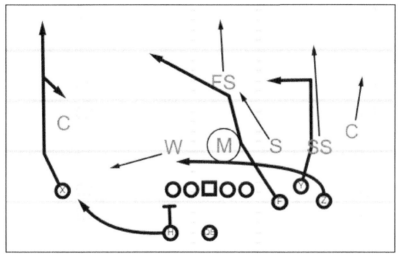

In either diagram, if the Sam carries hard inside, the dig route will open up as the last read in the progression.

This concept was almost exclusively used on third downs. The Packers most often saw five man pressures and tight man coverage when they called this concept.

Why it Worked: The Packers hit the drive route twice vs

man coverage variations in week 2.

The Packers call the true empty version shown in the 2nd diagram against Chicago in week 12 for a third down conversion.

Why it Didn't Work: The drive route opens up in week one against man under two deep, but MVS drops the ball. This clip shows how the man defender has to fight through four bodies to stay with his receiver.

Pin

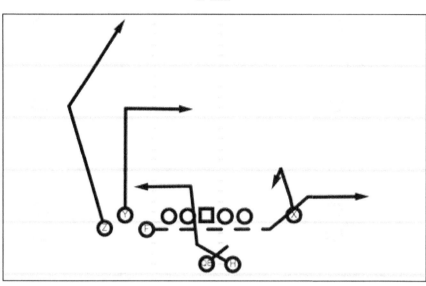

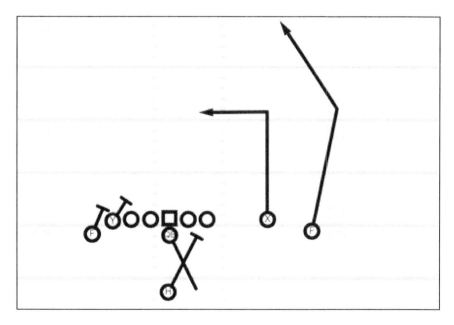

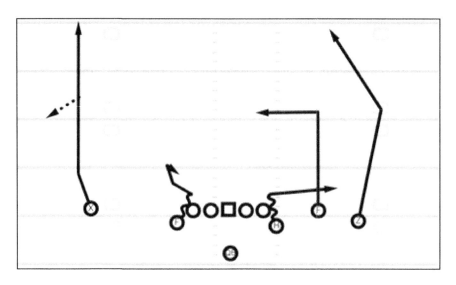

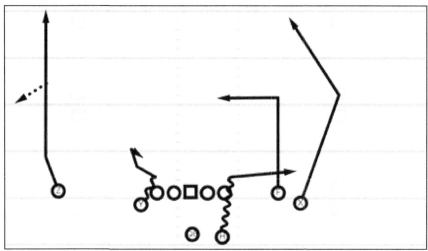

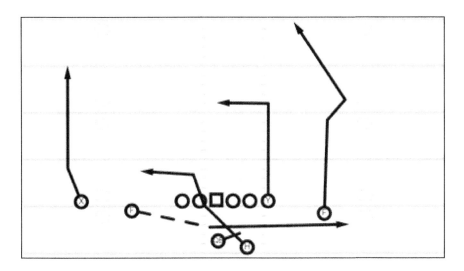

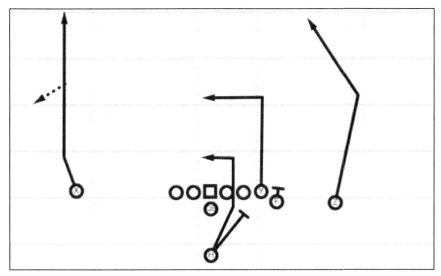

Average Yards per Play	12.7

1st Down		3rd/4th Down (includes RZ)	
Called	Average	Called	Success Rate
2	26.0	2	50%
2nd Down 6-1		**2nd Down 7+**	
Called	Average	Called	Average
1	0.0	1	0.0
Red Zone 10-0		**Red Zone 10-20**	
Called	Touchdown %	Called	Touchdown %
0	0%	0	0%

Cover 1		Cover 2		Cover 0	
Called	Average	Called	Average	Called	Average
1	24.0	0	0	0	0
Cover 3		**Cover 4**		**Cover 42**	
Called	Average	Called	Average	Called	Average
2	0.0	0	0	1	52.0
Cover 5		**Drop 8**		**5 Man Pressure**	
Called	Average	Called	Average	Called	Average
1	0.0	0	0	1	0.0

Week	Quarter	Time	Down	ToGo	Location	Yards
Week 6 vs TB	2	3:49	2	3	GNB 32	0
Week 6 vs TB	3	10:55	3	5	GNB 30	0
Week 9 vs SF	2	2:00	1	10	GNB 48	52
Week 12 vs CHI	3	6:09	3	10	GNB 34	24
Week 17 vs CHI	3	13:27	1	10	GNB 47	0
DIV vs LAR	4	13:37	2	7	RAM 47	0

Similar to the Middle Read – Dagger concept, the Pin concept allows the Packers to isolate Adams as the X receiver to run fades/comebacks/hinges. This use of personnel allows for progression carry over for the quarterback. If the X is one on one, work the X. If he is doubled, work the concept.

Typically against single high looks, the X will be isolated so the quarterback will work him in the 1 on 1.

If the defense brackets the X with a cover 4 / cover 2 style coverage, the numbers work for the Pin concept. Additionally, the post has big play potential against quarters when the safety takes #2 on his vertical release. The next image shows how the Pin concept can take advantage of quarters coverage.

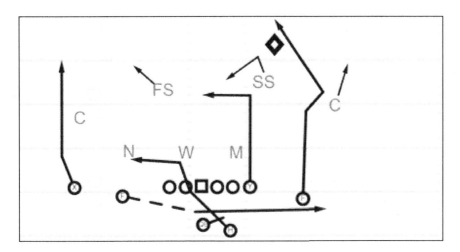

The use of the tight split for the post route helps gain inside leverage without asking the receiver to break a DB's leverage from a normal split. With his tight split, the CB will typically align outside based on his divider rules.

Why it Worked: In week 12, Rodgers works the dig route against cover 1 with a bracket on the X receiver (Adams). With a bracket on the X receiver, there is no rat/hole player to help on the inside break of a dig route. This is yet another example of the Packers using Adams in an isolated

X receiver position to declare coverage and open up the rest of the progression for Rodgers.

This is also the case in week 17, except the Bears bring a five man rush and use the free safety to get over the top of Adams. This leaves the post route open for a home run shot. MVS drops an easy touchdown on this play.

Why it Didn't Work: The Packers call the version in the first diagram in DIV vs LAR. Rodgers works past an open Adams on the snag route and forces the ball to the covered check down.

Verticals (Traditional)

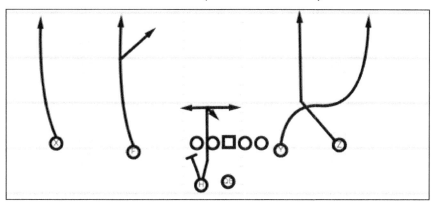

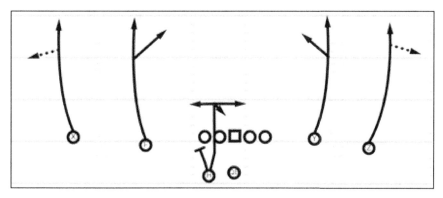

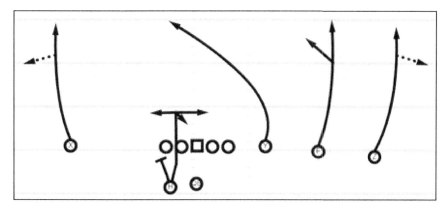

Average Yards per Play	6.6

1st Down		3rd/4th Down (includes RZ)	
Called	Average	Called	Success Rate
9	-0.5	9	44%
2nd Down 6-1		**2nd Down 7+**	
Called	Average	Called	Average
1	7.0	4	12.3
Red Zone 10-0		**Red Zone 10-20**	
Called	Touchdown %	Called	Touchdown %
0	0%	0	0%

Cover 1		Cover 2		Cover 0	
Called	Average	Called	Average	Called	Average
3	19.0	8	8.0	2	6.0
Cover 3		**Cover 4**		**Cover 42**	
Called	Average	Called	Average	Called	Average
4	4.5	3	0.0	1	-11.0
Cover 5		**Drop 8**		**5 Man Pressure**	
Called	Average	Called	Average	Called	Average
1	0.0	0	0	1	0.0

Week	Quarter	Time	Down	ToGo	Location	Yards
Week 1 vs MN	1	1:52	3	5	GNB 44	12
Week 1 vs MN	2	0:25	1	10	MIN 45	0
Week 1 vs MN	2	0:21	2	10	MIN 45	45
Week 2 vs DET	3	9:30	3	20	DET 28	-11
Week 4 vs ATL	4	6:40	3	25	ATL 43	13
Week 6 vs TB	1	6:51	3	7	GNB 23	11
Week 6 vs TB	2	10:57	2	10	GNB 25	0
Week 6 vs TB	2	0:30	1	10	GNB 39	0
Week 7 vs HOU	2	2:06	1	10	GNB 46	0
Week 7 vs HOU	3	4:51	3	4	HTX 45	45
Week 7 vs HOU	4	9:44	3	10	GNB 21	0
Week 8 vs MIN	3	1:28	1	30	GNB 48	0
Week 8 vs MIN	4	5:31	2	5	GNB 31	7
Week 9 vs SF	2	0:44	1	10	GNB 26	-11
Week 10 vs JAX	4	12:01	3	9	GNB 26	23
Week 10 vs JAX	4	11:17	1	10	GNB 49	7
Week 11 vs IND	1	0:09	1	20	GNB 15	TO
Week 11 vs IND	2	0:42	1	10	GNB 36	0
Week 13 vs PHI	4	5:04	3	10	GNB 22	0
Week 14 vs DET	2	1:00	1	10	GNB 35	0
DIV vs LAR	3	7:44	3	8	GNB 42	0
NFCCG vs TB	2	2:00	2	10	GNB 13	4
NFCCG vs TB	2	0:34	2	17	GNB 33	0

The Four Vertical concept is a part of the Packers situational package for two minute drills and end of game scenarios.

The four vertical concept creates an evenly spaced attack down the field for the quarterback. Against single high coverage, the quarterback has 1 on 1 matchups on the outside or he can work the slot receivers away from the lean of the free safety help. Against two high, the slot receivers will bend across the safeties' face to create more space and leverage for the outside receivers while trying to work themselves open inside.

Running backs are often given freedom with their check down routes on this concept. They can work in/out against tight man or they can settle over the ball vs a soft zone.

Why it Worked: In week 7, it appears Rodgers checks to a vertical concept on the front side to get Adams on a seam route against man coverage. Rodgers gets Adams 1 on 1 for a touchdown.

Why it Didn't Work: The Packers often reserved this concept for two minute or end of game situations. In these situations, the verticals become harder to hit. This was often the case for the Packers with this play call.

Four Verticals Variations (RB Seams)

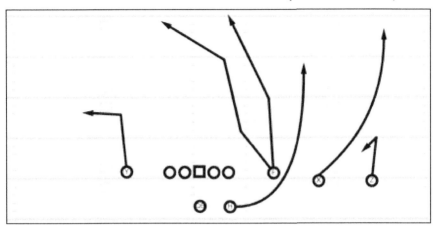

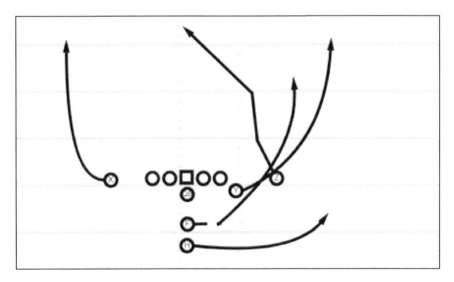

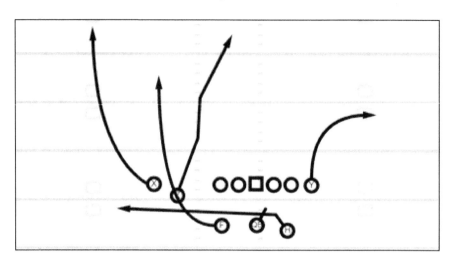

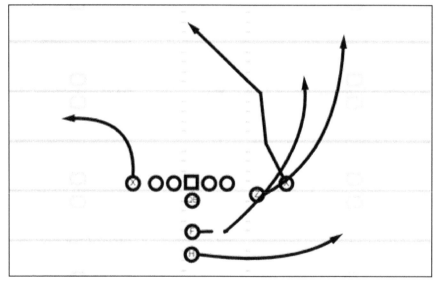

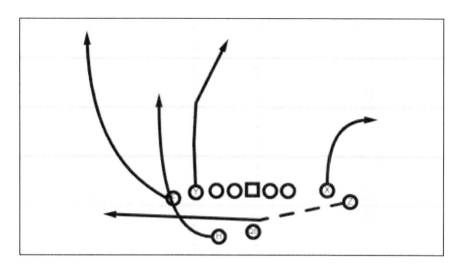

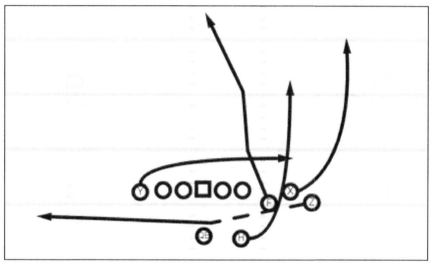

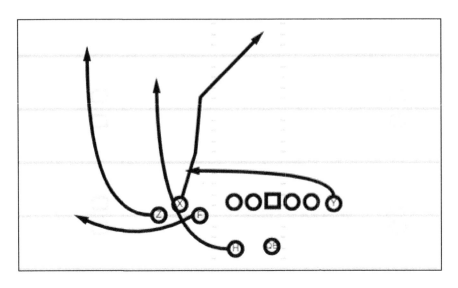

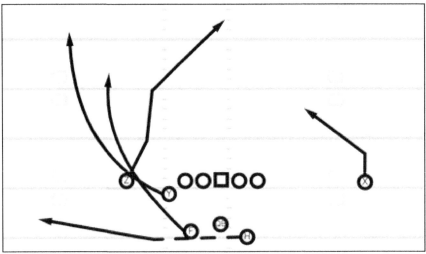

Average Yards per Play	9.4

1st Down		3rd/4th Down (includes RZ)	
Called	Average	Called	Success Rate
13	10.8	1	0%
2nd Down 6-1		2nd Down 7+	
Called	Average	Called	Average
3	11.3	5	6.2
Red Zone 10-0		Red Zone 10-20	
Called	Touchdown %	Called	Touchdown %
0	0%	0	0%

Cover 1		Cover 2		Cover 0	
Called	Average	Called	Average	Called	Average
1	5.0	8	10.0	0	0
Cover 3		Cover 4		Cover 42	
Called	Average	Called	Average	Called	Average
7	11.0	3	5.7	0	0
Cover 5		Drop 8		5 Man Pressure	
Called	Average	Called	Average	Called	Average
1	0.0	1	0.0	2	13.5

Week	Quarter	Time	Down	ToGo	Location	Yards
Week 1 vs MN	1	13:24	1	10	GNB 36	6
Week 1 vs MN	1	9:40	1	10	MIN 25	15
Week 2 vs DET	1	5:56	2	3	DET 25	0
Week 3 vs NO	4	15:00	1	10	GNB 39	5
Week 3 vs NO	4	6:36	1	10	GNB 36	23
Week 4 vs ATL	1	13:28	2	10	GNB 27	27
Week 4 vs ATL	1	8:17	2	1	GNB 43	29
Week 4 vs ATL	2	5:36	1	10	ATL 47	0
Week 6 vs TB	1	10:38	3	8	TAM 21	0
Week 7 vs HOU	2	9:36	1	10	GNB 17	31
Week 7 vs HOU	3	3:10	2	10	GNB 24	0
Week 8 vs MIN	1	11:41	2	1	MIN 38	5
Week 11 vs IND	1	14:17	1	10	CLT 46	8
Week 11 vs IND	1	5:39	1	10	GNB 34	0
Week 11 vs IND	4	8:52	1	10	GNB 23	9
Week 12 vs CHI	1	11:39	1	10	CHI 39	5
Week 16 vs TEN	1	13:40	1	10	GNB 50	8
Week 16 vs TEN	1	3:41	2	9	GNB 36	-1
DIV vs LAR	2	6:16	2	14	RAM 25	12
DIV vs LAR	3	0:10	1	10	GNB 39	7
NFCCG vs TB	1	2:29	2	8	GNB 12	-7
NFCCG vs TB	3	11:52	1	10	GNB 42	24

Matt LaFleur and the Packers adopted the in-vogue Four Vertical – RB Seam concept as a staple part of their offense in 2020. Usually with some play action and misdirection, this action is a nice way to create added leverage and space down the field on a traditional concept.

The Chiefs popularized this concept in the NFL in 2017 with their opening game victory over the Patriots. Over the last few seasons various teams have sprinkled the concept in, but few have committed to it like the Packers did in 2020. Especially among the Shanahan disciples.

The play action and misdirection elements are to try and open up one of the two interior seam routes. Communication between hook players is placed at a premium. Who carries the seam routes in a single high structure? If this can not be figured out in a second or two, the offense has a seam runner open downfield as the first read in the progression.

Defenses did a nice job covering up the two seam routes in 2020. The Packers made this concept successful by working the back side isolation Omaha/Slant, the cover 2 turkey hole shot, and the check down. This concept became versatile as a true way to attack with all five eligible.

The back side slant or Omaha route is a nice quick first read for a the quarterback against a pressure look or when the defense rotates hard with the motion to the vertical side. Most often Adams would be lined up as the isolated back side receiver. Against the Rams, Rodgers hits Adams on the slant route. The Rams stay in a two high look after the motion, and the weak hook player bumps hard leaving a big slant window for Adams.

The early week 11 clip shows Rodgers hitting the Omaha route against a cover three shell that rotates hard with the jet motion.

Why it Worked: Aaron Rodgers was able to quickly recognize Cover 2 to hit the "turkey Hole" between the corner and safety on a few occasions in 2020. Once in the NFCCG and once in week 4. In week 11 it was open, but the throw and timing was slightly off to force an incompletion.

When the seams were not open, Rodgers was able to get the ball to the check down in the flat relatively quickly. The hook defenders would often turn and run with the vertical releases, leaving a ton of room for the check down.

Why it Didn't Work: In week 16, the Titans rotate their cover 3 strong with the fake jet motion. This frees up the flat defender to trigger on the check down when it is thrown.

Over -Curl/Swirl

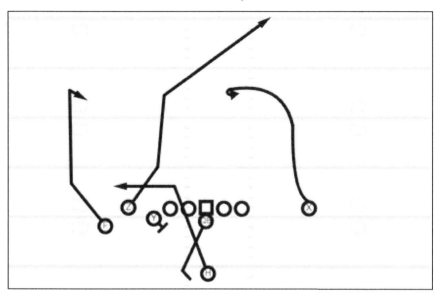

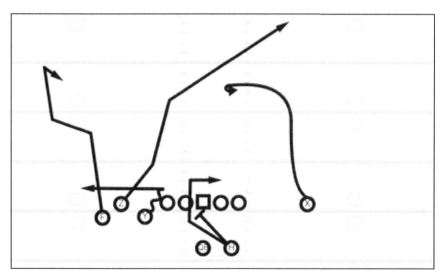

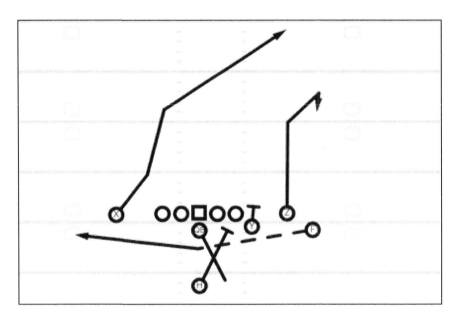

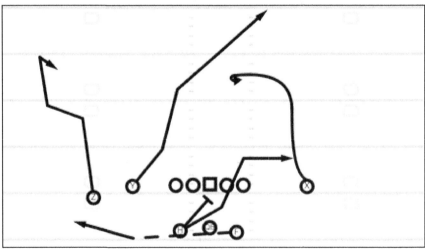

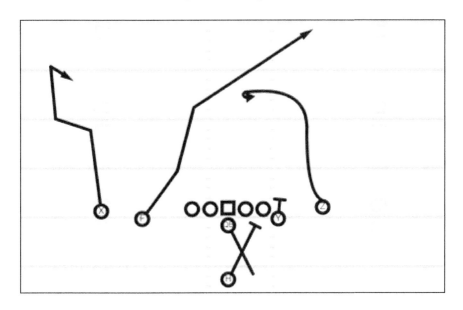

Average Yards per Play	14.3

1st Down		3rd/4th Down (includes RZ)	
Called	Average	Called	Success Rate
2	2.5	4	25%
2nd Down 6-1		**2nd Down 7+**	
Called	Average	Called	Average
1	0.0	1	45.0
Red Zone 10-0		**Red Zone 10-20**	
Called	Touchdown %	Called	Touchdown %
0	0%	0	0%

Cover 1		Cover 2		Cover 0	
Called	Average	Called	Average	Called	Average
0	0	0	0	0	0
Cover 3		**Cover 4**		**Cover 42**	
Called	Average	Called	Average	Called	Average
4	1.3	4	27.3	0	0
Cover 5		**Drop 8**		**5 Man Pressure**	
Called	Average	Called	Average	Called	Average
0	0	0	0	0	0

Week	Quarter	Time	Down	ToGo	Location	Yards
Week 3 vs NO	3	15:00	1	10	GNB 25	0
Week 3 vs NO	3	14:50	3	10	GNB 25	72
Week 6 vs TB	2	10:53	3	10	GNB 25	0
Week 6 vs TB	3	7:04	2	3	GNB 41	0
Week 8 vs MIN	3	9:04	2	17	GNB 18	45
Week 13 vs PHI	4	6:55	3	12	GNB 21	0
Week 15 vs CAR	2	7:29	1	10	CAR 47	5
NFCCG vs TB	1	8:23	3	9	GNB 43	-8

The Over – Curl/Swirl concept is a shot play designed to attack cover 4 teams. Greg Cosell did a fantastic break down of this concept on the NFL Matchup Show during the season, illustrating with how it attacks quarters coverage.

The design of the concept is to occupy both the weak safety and weak corner with the route of the X receiver. The next diagram shows how the bracket of the X receiver opens up the deep over route.

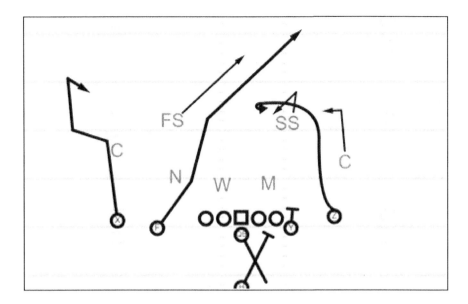

Against single high, the deep over must cross the middle safety's face. Many single high man or match style coverages will lock the weak corner on a vertical release from the X, leaving a lot of space over his head if the deep over can win vs the middle safety. The spacing for this concept works much better on the high school or college hashes against single high, as the spacing allows for the deep over to cross the safety's face easier.

The most important coaching point for this concept against cover 4/cover 7 is the X receiver to occupy both the safety and corner. He must not break his route too early inside. If he breaks it too early inside, the corner might fall back to his deep quarter if the defense is playing Cone (Saban check).

Why it Worked: With the weak safety bracketing the X receiver with the corner, the deep over route is able to win inside the strong safety for a big gain. All it takes is one false step inside for the weak corner for him not to get back into his quarter in a "Cone" call.

Why it Didn't Work: On the week 3 incompletion, the Saints are poaching with the weak safety. This means the weak safety will look to the strong side of the formation and take away the deep over route from leverage.

In the NFCCG, the Bucs play Saban's "7 Switch" to the three man surface and a "Cone" bracket on Adams at the X receiver spot. The weak corner and safety play the Cone bracket perfectly and the Curl is passed off to the safety. This allows the corner to help on the deep over with leverage. Additionally, the nickel gets a good jam on the deep over route too which gives the corner time to make up ground.

PA Keeper Slide-Delay

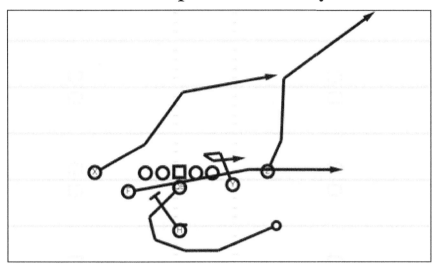

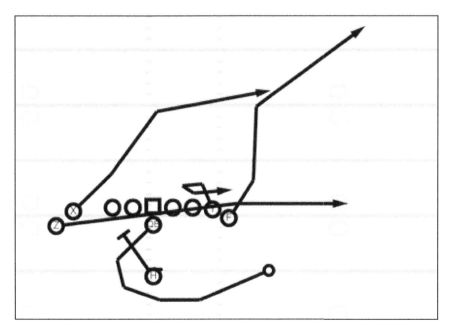

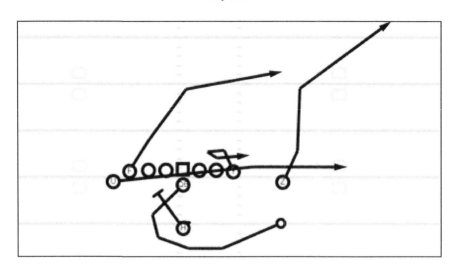

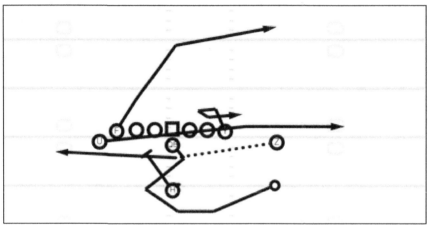

190

Average Yards per Play		5.5	

1st Down		3rd/4th Down (includes RZ)	
Called	Average	Called	Success Rate
3	6.3	3	100%
2nd Down 6-1		**2nd Down 7+**	
Called	Average	Called	Average
3	3.7	3	4.3
Red Zone 10-0		**Red Zone 10-20**	
Called	Touchdown %	Called	Touchdown %
1	0%	1	0%

Cover 1		Cover 2		Cover 0	
Called	Average	Called	Average	Called	Average
3	3.7	5	3.6	0	0
Cover 3		**Cover 4**		**Cover 42**	
Called	Average	Called	Average	Called	Average
2	6.5	0	0	0	0
Cover 5		**Drop 8**		**5 Man Pressure**	
Called	Average	Called	Average	Called	Average
0	0	0	0	2	8.0

Week	Quarter	Time	Down	ToGo	Location	Yards
Week 6 vs TB	2	12:58	2	10	GNB 22	0
Week 8 vs MIN	1	14:24	2	6	GNB 29	8
Week 8 vs MIN	1	9:09	4	1	MIN 24	13
Week 9 vs SF	2	2:25	2	8	GNB 37	11
Week 11 vs IND	1	11:06	3	1	CLT 42	4
Week 11 vs IND	1	10:29	1	10	CLT 38	4
Week 11 vs IND	2	8:27	1	10	CLT 17	12
Week 12 vs CHI	1	13:03	2	9	CHI 49	2
Week 13 vs PHI	4	7:47	1	10	GNB 23	3
Week 13 vs PHI	4	1:38	3	4	GNB 40	5
Week 14 vs DET	4	1:40	3	5	DET 40	6
Week 15 vs CAR	2	14:20	2	6	CAR 6	0
Week 17 vs CHI	4	7:30	2	2	CHI 43	3

The Slide-Delay Keeper is my personal favorite Keeper variation. The play gets two underneath threats horizontally spaced for the quarterback, with a low crossing route over the top. When the threat of the QB run is included, this concept creates four options for the quarterback in his immediate vision off of misdirection action.

The "Slide" route references the flat route coming from behind the line of scrimmage from the opposite side of the ball.

The "Delay" route references the play side TE blocking the defensive end before slow releasing for an outlet for the quarterback late.

Against man coverage teams, the versions with he Z receiver working on the slide route work well, as a man defender has to work his way through all of the linebackers to get to the other side of the field.

Why it Worked: The Packers were very efficient with this concept on 3rd and 4th downs. In week 8, Rodgers hits the delay route. Rodgers keeps it for a first down in week 11, and hits the slide route in week 13 and week 14. The two underneath routes combined with the threat of the QB run create a nice triple threat in short yardage situations.

The Packers liked this play call against the fast flowing defense of the Colts in week 11. The misdirection against fast flow defenses creates easier leverage on the routes working away from the run action.

Why it Didn't Work: In general, the concept was very

efficient for the Packers. Somebody was usually open on each occasion it was called.

In week 15, Rodgers doesn't find the open delay route and throws the ball away instead.

PA Keeper Slide

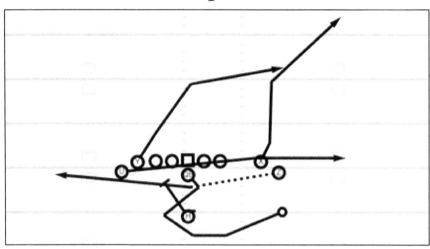

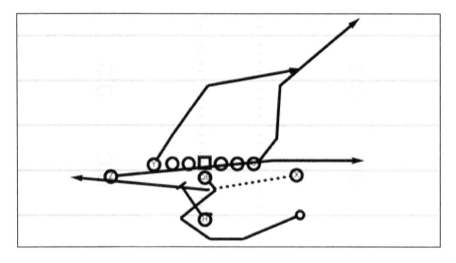

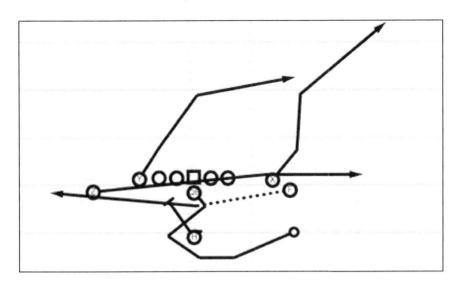

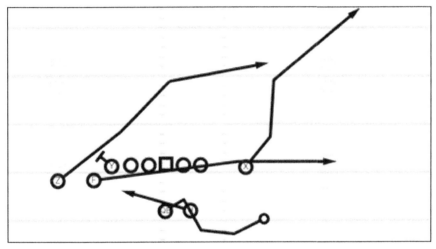

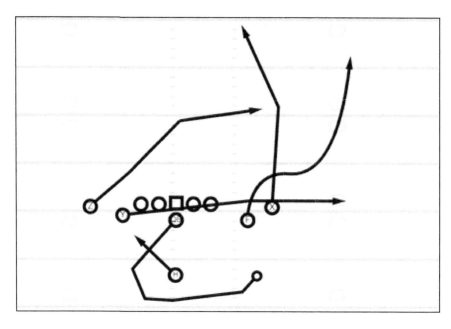

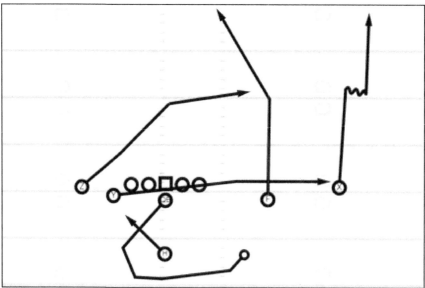

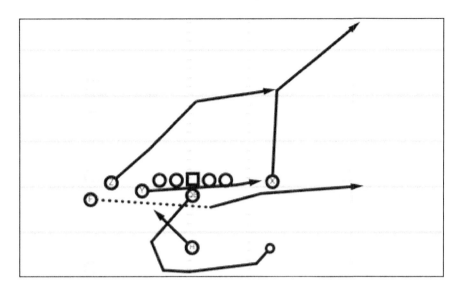

Average Yards per Play	7.8

1st Down		3rd/4th Down (includes RZ)	
Called	Average	Called	Success Rate
18	8.1	0	0%
2nd Down 6-1		**2nd Down 7+**	
Called	Average	Called	Average
6	4.3	1	24.0
Red Zone 10-0		**Red Zone 10-20**	
Called	Touchdown %	Called	Touchdown %
2	100%	0	0%

Cover 1		Cover 2		Cover 0	
Called	Average	Called	Average	Called	Average
3	13.0	1	13.0	1	2.0
Cover 3		**Cover 4**		**Cover 42**	
Called	Average	Called	Average	Called	Average
11	9.0	1	14.0	2	5.0
Cover 5		**Drop 8**		**5 Man Pressure**	
Called	Average	Called	Average	Called	Average
0	0	0	0	6	3.3

Week	Quarter	Time	Down	ToGo	Location	Yards
Week 2 vs DET	1	7:04	2	6	DET 42	0
Week 2 vs DET	3	10:35	2	6	DET 32	14
Week 3 vs NO	1	12:35	2	6	GNB 35	9
Week 3 vs NO	3	5:55	1	10	GNB 25	16
Week 3 vs NO	3	0:33	1	10	GNB 25	14
Week 3 vs NO	4	14:16	2	5	GNB 44	0
Week 3 vs NO	4	10:55	1	10	NOR 47	12
Week 7 vs HOU	1	7:15	1	10	GNB 20	0
Week 7 vs HOU	2	13:38	2	3	HTX 3	3
Week 7 vs HOU	3	6:55	1	10	GNB 39	5
Week 8 vs MIN	1	11:16	1	10	MIN 33	4
Week 8 vs MIN	3	5:52	1	10	GNB 25	0
Week 10 vs JAX	3	10:26	1	10	GNB 25	4
Week 10 vs JAX	3	2:43	1	10	GNB 20	31
Week 11 vs IND	3	1:54	1	10	GNB 22	3
Week 12 vs CHI	2	8:58	1	10	CHI 36	4
Week 12 vs CHI	2	4:40	1	2	CHI 2	2
Week 13 vs PHI	1	0:35	2	9	GNB 13	24
Week 14 vs DET	1	6:12	1	10	GNB 31	10
Week 16 vs TEN	1	12:19	1	10	OTI 30	13
Week 16 vs TEN	1	1:22	1	10	OTI 47	17
Week 16 vs TEN	1	0:37	1	10	OTI 30	0
Week 17 vs CHI	1	2:37	1	10	CHI 30	4
DIV vs LAR	1	1:20	1	10	GNB 47	6
DIV vs LAR	3	0:58	2	6	GNB 30	0

In general, this concept is another easy-completion style concept in the Packers offense. The Keeper with just the slide route is more of a true naked with the defensive end usually unblocked.

My favorite version of this concept is shown in the fifth diagram. Against single high coverage, the front side post-wheel will pull out the corner and flat defender. This places the hook player in a run-pass conflict with the slide route. A good clip of this can be seen in week 8. The Packers also ran this version twice in week 3 for completions of 14 and 12 yards.

The next diagram shows how the slide route can open up with this action.

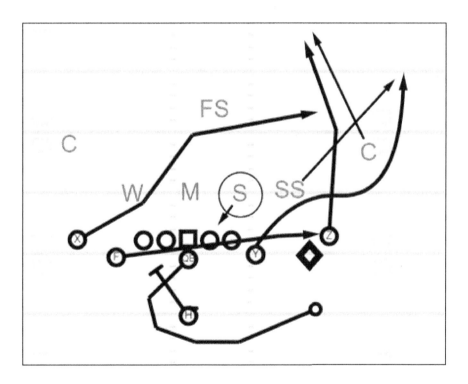

LaFleur and the Packers are good about incorporating double moves into their base concepts. Using a double move within the Keeper package is a good way to keep the play side #1 receiver a part of the progression of the play. The quarterback can peek this route without having to commit to it, while still being on time for the slide and crossing routes.

Why it Worked: The misdirection fake jet motion added for the slide route opened up for a few big gains. The Packers worked the slide route against the Lions' man coverage in week 2. The slide route is hard to follow in man coverage, whether it is the off-ball tight end or a wide receiver coming across.

The big gainer in week 10 shows Rodgers hitting the low crossing route.

Why it Didn't Work: On the week 16 incompletion, the Titans use their free safety to cut the slide route. The defensive end was able to get quick pressure on Rodgers as well to force the throwaway with he first outlet covered up.

PA Keeper Delay/Add

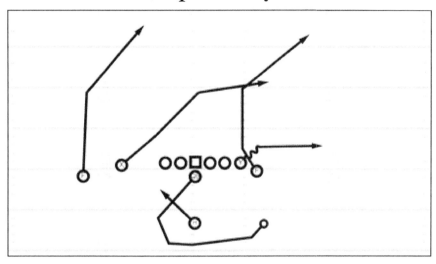

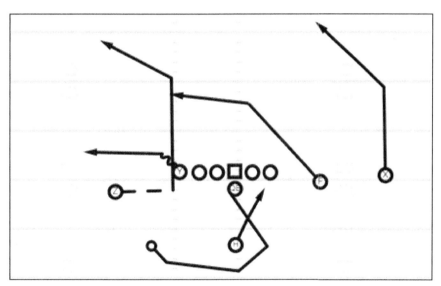

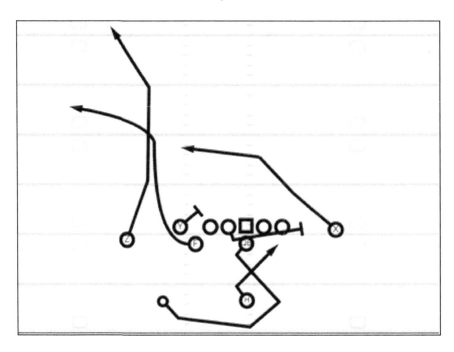

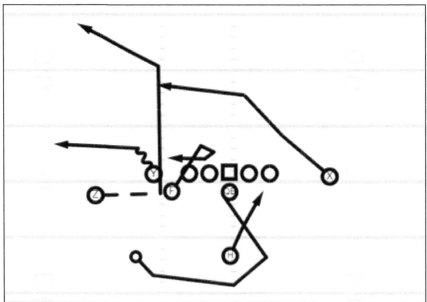

Average Yards per Play	6.8

1st Down		3rd/4th Down (includes RZ)	
Called	Average	Called	Success Rate
4	5.8	1	0%
2nd Down 6-1		**2nd Down 7+**	
Called	Average	Called	Average
4	8.3	1	12.0
Red Zone 10-0		**Red Zone 10-20**	
Called	Touchdown %	Called	Touchdown %
0	0%	0	0%

Cover 1		Cover 2		Cover 0	
Called	Average	Called	Average	Called	Average
2	4.0	1	3.0	0	0
Cover 3		**Cover 4**		**Cover 42**	
Called	Average	Called	Average	Called	Average
4	10.3	0	0	0	0
Cover 5		**Drop 8**		**5 Man Pressure**	
Called	Average	Called	Average	Called	Average
0	0	0	0	3	5.3

Week	Quarter	Time	Down	ToGo	Location	Yards
Week 4 vs ATL	4	3:38	1	10	GNB 26	4
Week 4 vs ATL	4	2:00	3	9	ATL 44	0
Week 11 vs IND	1	9:48	2	6	CLT 34	8
Week 14 vs DET	3	1:11	2	1	DET 37	3
Week 17 vs CHI	3	14:13	2	6	GNB 32	15
DIV vs LAR	1	2:32	1	10	GNB 33	9
DIV vs LAR	4	4:14	2	9	RAM 45	12
NFCCG vs TB	1	0:32	1	10	GNB 43	5
NFCCG vs TB	3	5:09	2	5	TAM 39	7
NFCCG vs TB	3	4:30	1	10	TAM 32	5

This version of the Keeper concept aims to get the ball to the first tight end in the flat. After setting on the defensive end, he will shed and gain outside leverage to the flat.

This route and block is meant to simulate the backside seal off on inside/outside zone. As this block can often be a tough block for a tight end, this Keeper will give the back side defensive end hesitation on zone concepts and the tight end will have an easier time protecting C gap going forward.

The two man front side flood/scissors corner call can be seen in weeks 4 and 11.

Rodgers hits this route in all three NFCCG clips.

Why it Worked: The week 17 completion shows an easy flat route to the tight end. He sets on the end man on the line of scrimmage, then sheds him after the play fake and gets outside. Quick accurate throw from Rodgers.

Why it Didn't Work: The only incompletion on this concept came in week 4 at the end of the game on a third and long.

PA Keeper C.P.

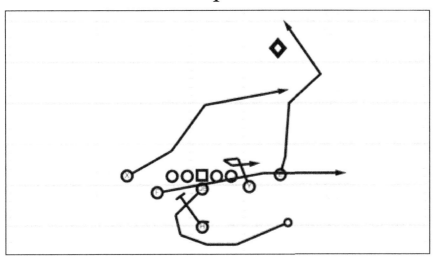

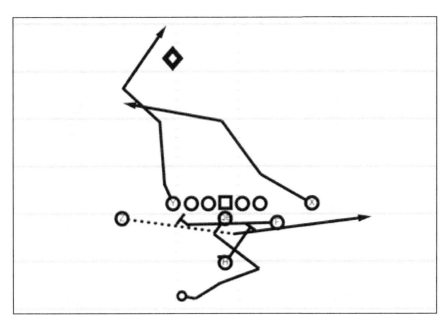

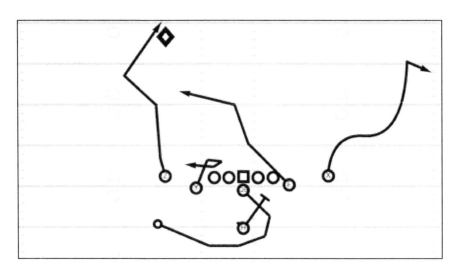

Average Yards per Play	7.3

1st Down		3rd/4th Down (includes RZ)	
Called	Average	Called	Success Rate
4	0.0	0	0%
2nd Down 6-1		**2nd Down 7+**	
Called	Average	Called	Average
1	8.0	1	36.0
Red Zone 10-0		**Red Zone 10-20**	
Called	Touchdown %	Called	Touchdown %
0	0%	0	0%

Cover 1		Cover 2		Cover 0	
Called	Average	Called	Average	Called	Average
1	36.0	0	0	0	0
Cover 3		**Cover 4**		**Cover 42**	
Called	Average	Called	Average	Called	Average
2	0.0	2	4.0	1	0.0
Cover 5		**Drop 8**		**5 Man Pressure**	
Called	Average	Called	Average	Called	Average
0	0	0	0	0	0

Week	Quarter	Time	Down	ToGo	Location	Yards
Week 12 vs CHI	2	12:24	1	10	GNB 20	0
Week 12 vs CHI	3	8:06	2	6	CHI 49	8
Week 13 vs PHI	2	4:00	2	9	GNB 19	36
Week 13 vs PHI	2	3:12	1	10	PHI 45	0
Week 15 vs CAR	2	3:28	1	10	GNB 25	0
NFCCG vs TB	4	12:20	1	10	GNB 19	0

The C.P. (Corner-Post) tag on the Keeper concept is designed to make a free safety pay for cutting a low crosser. The C.P. runner should be able to win inside leverage on his man.

Why it Worked: With the corner and free safety doubling Adams on the C.P. in week 13, Rodgers hits the tight end on the low cross for a big gain behind the linebackers.

Why it Didn't Work: In the NFCCG, the Bucs bring a nickel edge pressure that forces Rodgers off his spot early. The Bucs double Adams on the C.P. route and the low cross opens up late.

PA Double Cross (& non PA)

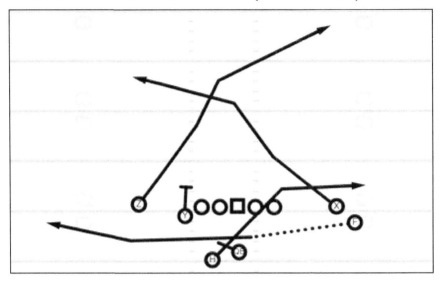

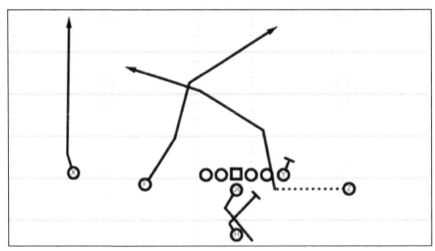

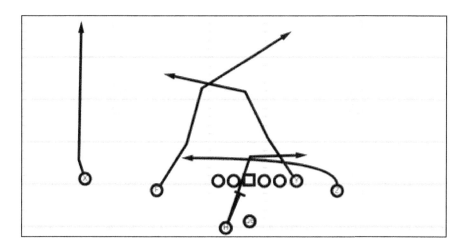

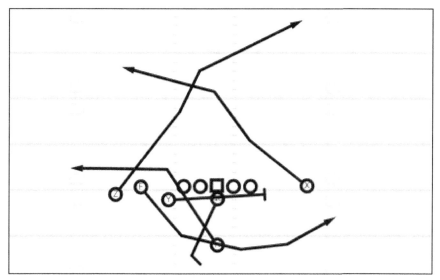

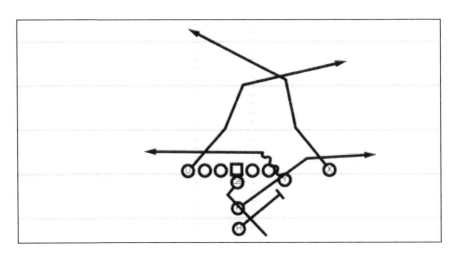

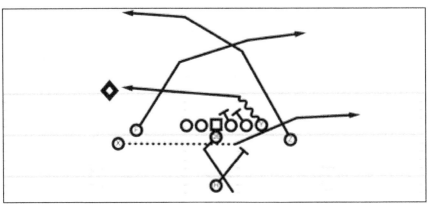

Average Yards per Play	9.2

1st Down		3rd/4th Down (includes RZ)	
Called	Average	Called	Success Rate
5	9.2	3	67%
2nd Down 6-1		**2nd Down 7+**	
Called	Average	Called	Average
4	12.8	3	0.0
Red Zone 10-0		**Red Zone 10-20**	
Called	Touchdown %	Called	Touchdown %
6	50%	0	0%

Cover 1		Cover 2		Cover 0	
Called	Average	Called	Average	Called	Average
8	7.5	1	0.0	1	3.0
Cover 3		**Cover 4**		**Cover 42**	
Called	Average	Called	Average	Called	Average
2	18.0	1	5.0	0	0
Cover 5		**Drop 8**		**5 Man Pressure**	
Called	Average	Called	Average	Called	Average
0	0	0	0	3	12.3

Week	Quarter	Time	Down	ToGo	Location	Yards
Week 3 vs NO	2	10:36	2	5	NOR 5	5
Week 3 vs NO	3	13:08	3	1	NOR 1	0
Week 4 vs ATL	4	3:24	3	1	GNB 35	20
Week 7 vs HOU	2	15:00	2	2	HTX 41	36
Week 8 vs MIN	3	3:49	2	9	GNB 50	0
Week 12 vs CHI	3	6:38	2	10	GNB 33	0
Week 13 vs PHI	2	2:00	1	10	PHI 31	5
Week 14 vs DET	3	13:34	1	20	GNB 23	14
Week 14 vs DET	3	7:13	1	10	DET 10	0
Week 14 vs DET	4	12:07	1	4	DET 4	4
Week 14 vs DET	4	3:47	2	9	DET 34	0
Week 15 vs CAR	1	10:46	2	4	CAR 8	7
Week 16 vs TEN	2	15:00	3	1	OTI 21	21
Week 16 vs TEN	2	9:01	1	10	GNB 45	23
Week 17 vs CHI	2	15:00	2	3	CHI 3	3

This concept is a great way to combat the "Dropkick/Top/Cut" call where a free safety will cut a crossing route to gain leverage back for a defense. With two crossing route, the free safety in a single high structure now has to choose which one to cut. With the higher crossing route appearing first, this is often the route the free safety leverages. Unless the corner on the high cross recognizes this quickly, the low cross will have open range on the other side of the field. A key coaching point for the high cross is to not cross the hash too quickly to keep the corner high and off the low cross. Stay vertical and "take two", occupy your corner and the free safety.

The Packers would often scheme this route for Adams. The next image shows the single high FS dropkick/cut response from the defense, leaving the X receiver with a clear picture on the other side of the field.

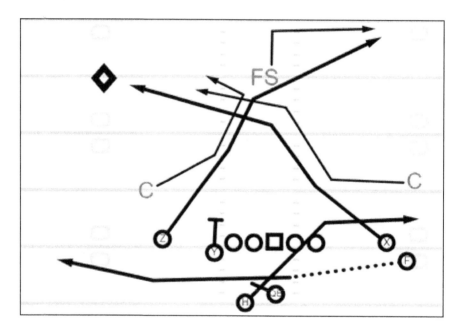

The 2nd diagram shows a version off of the Packers Duo concept. The short motion from the Z will make the defense think he is digging out the strong safety, leaving the corner unblocked. Defenses that are well-prepared for the Packers run game will have the corner insert aggressively into he run fit vs this look. If the Packers see this from the press box, the will call this version of double cross and the corner will be in a trail position once he realizes it is play action.

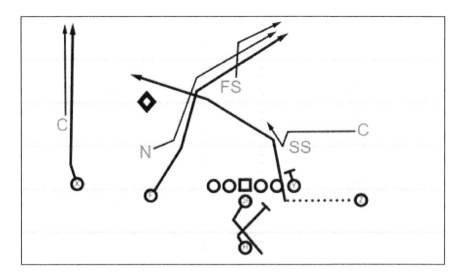

The Packers will also run the concept in their drop back game. The 3ʳᵈ diagram shows this variation.

Why it Worked: The 5ᵗʰ diagram shows a short yardage variation used in week 4 to convert a 3ʳᵈ & 1. The Y tight end gets lost against man coverage working across the formation.

The week 7 clip shows text book teach tape for the concept. The Texans play cover 1 and the safety attempts to cut the high crosser, leaving Adams on the low crosser 1 on 1. He gets a great release at the line of scrimmage vs press coverage as well, getting the DB to turn his hips to the outside.

Why it Didn't Work: In week 12, the Bears disguise a two high trap with post snap rotation. The corner traps the low cross late breaking up the play with a big hit.

PA Bang Dig

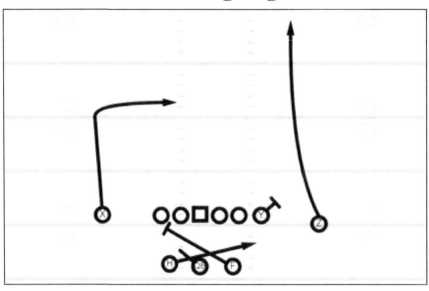

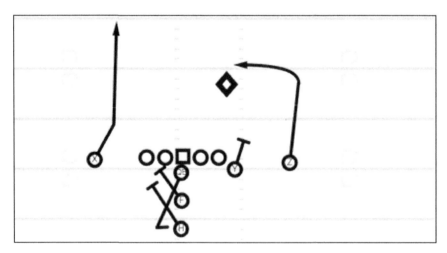

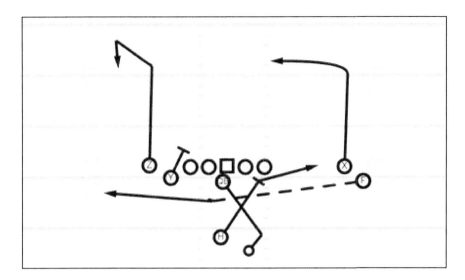

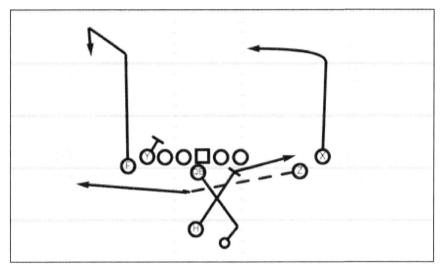

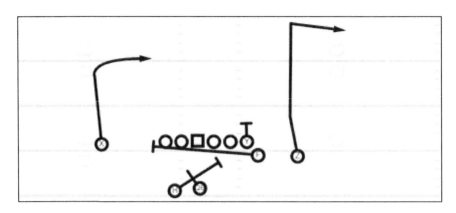

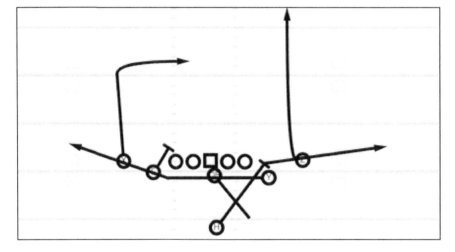

Average Yards per Play	7.5

1st Down		3rd/4th Down (includes RZ)	
Called	Average	Called	Success Rate
11	7.3	0	0%
2nd Down 6-1		**2nd Down 7+**	
Called	Average	Called	Average
2	9.0	2	7.0
Red Zone 10-0		**Red Zone 10-20**	
Called	Touchdown %	Called	Touchdown %
0	0%	0	0%

Cover 1		Cover 2		Cover 0	
Called	Average	Called	Average	Called	Average
3	2.3	1	0.0	0	0
Cover 3		**Cover 4**		**Cover 42**	
Called	Average	Called	Average	Called	Average
7	9.9	1	15.0	0	0
Cover 5		**Drop 8**		**5 Man Pressure**	
Called	Average	Called	Average	Called	Average
0	0	0	0	3	7.0

Week	Quarter	Time	Down	ToGo	Location	Yards
Week 1 vs MN	1	3:24	1	10	GNB 25	14
Week 2 vs DET	1	7:47	1	10	DET 46	4
Week 2 vs DET	2	4:06	2	6	GNB 33	17
Week 3 vs NO	1	5:07	1	10	GNB 25	10
Week 3 vs NO	2	3:42	1	10	GNB 35	0
Week 3 vs NO	3	14:54	2	10	GNB 25	0
Week 6 vs TB	2	13:07	1	10	GNB 22	0
Week 7 vs HOU	2	2:38	1	10	GNB 31	15
Week 7 vs HOU	3	5:36	1	10	GNB 49	6
Week 7 vs HOU	4	9:52	1	10	GNB 21	0
Week 8 vs MIN	2	11:37	2	9	MIN 45	14
Week 8 vs MIN	4	9:54	1	10	MIN 48	15
Week 12 vs CHI	3	12:29	1	10	GNB 18	5
Week 13 vs PHI	3	10:35	2	4	GNB 49	1
Week 16 vs TEN	3	9:23	1	10	GNB 26	11

The Bang concept is a staple 5-step play action route for the Shanahan/McVay/LaFleur coaching tree. The concept takes away a lot of reading and thinking for a quarterback. On base run downs, the concept works to attack the void created by linebackers fitting their run gaps.

The Bang route is a 5-7 step speed cut dig route. The main goal of the receiver is to win inside leverage vs the defender over him.

The play is ideal against single high coverage, as there isn't much safety help to drive on the bang route. Most of the Shanahan/McVay/LaFleur offenses will check out of the concept when presented with two high safeties, or check into it when given a single high safety.

The one completion against cover 4, Rodgers resets to the deep comeback as the second option on the progression when the bang window is closed. This clip can be found in week 8.

The Bang concept is a good way to feature your best receiver as the main option on a pass play. Off play action, the ball is almost certainly going to the receiver running the bang route. Adams had a lot of success with his route, mainly due to his ability to win inside leverage against a press corner.

Why it Worked: Rodgers hits Adams for a big play on the Bang route in week 2. From a tight split, Adams wins an inside release at the snap.

In week 3, Rodgers gets to the back side of the progression

and hits the Swirl route for a 10 yard gain

Why it Didn't Work: In week 6, the Bucs rotate late to cover 2 while bringing the nickel off the edge. The running back picks up the nickel, but the inside linebacker recovers into the Bang window nicely.

High Red Zone Specials

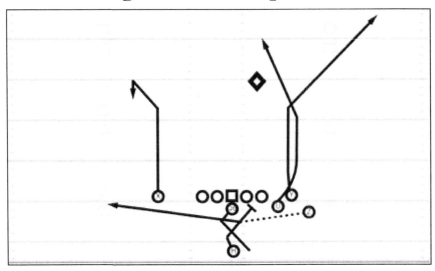

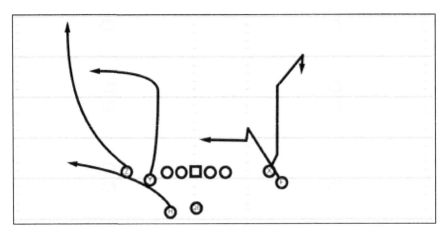

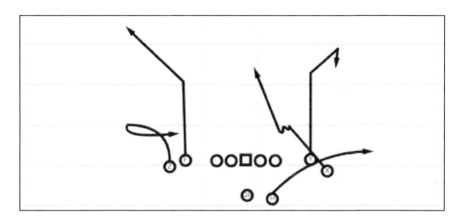

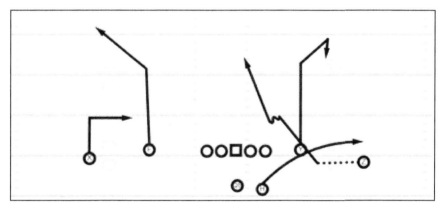

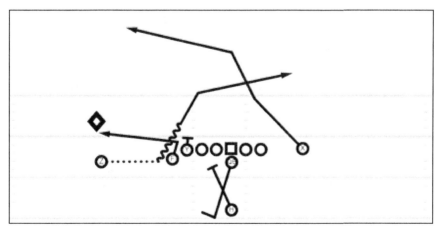

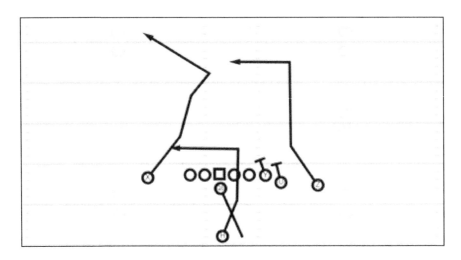

Average Yards per Play	12.3

1st Down		3rd/4th Down (includes RZ)	
Called	Average	Called	Success Rate
2	6.0	2	100%
2nd Down 6-1		**2nd Down 7+**	
Called	Average	Called	Average
1	7.0	2	18.0
Red Zone 10-0		**Red Zone 10-20**	
Called	Touchdown %	Called	Touchdown %
1	0%	5	60%

Cover 1		Cover 2		Cover 0	
Called	Average	Called	Average	Called	Average
2	9.0	2	18.5	0	0
Cover 3		**Cover 4**		**Cover 42**	
Called	Average	Called	Average	Called	Average
1	7.0	0	0	0	0
Cover 5		**Drop 8**		**5 Man Pressure**	
Called	Average	Called	Average	Called	Average
0	0	1	12.0	2	12.0

Week	Quarter	Time	Down	ToGo	Location	Yards
Week 2 vs DET	2	0:19	2	10	DET 11	11
Week 4 vs ATL	2	2:34	3	14	ATL 19	19
Week 11 vs IND	1	8:26	2	9	CLT 25	25
Week 12 vs CHI	1	7:31	3	10	CHI 12	12
Week 13 vs PHI	3	9:13	1	10	PHI 19	7
Week 15 vs CAR	1	10:46	2	4	CAR 8	7
Week 16 vs TEN	2	5:59	1	10	OTI 19	5

The Packers had a lot of red zone success in 2020. Through the use of creative concepts and great execution. LaFleur and Rodgers were able to maximize their efficiency in these areas.

This section focuses on high red zone concepts (outside the 10 yard line).

The first diagram shows a scissors variation used for a touchdown in week 11. The Colts played cover 2 and the tight end split the safeties for the touchdown.

The 3rd and 4th diagrams show "Snaggo" (snag-n-go) concepts. Both of these went for touchdowns, one in week 2 and one in week 12. The week 2 touchdown shows Rodgers hitting the Swirl route with perfect timing. The week 12 touchdown was a broken play after the Bears initially dropped 8 into coverage and covered up the concept.

Why it Worked: The 5th diagram shows a double cross variation used in week 15. The Z receiver picks the strong safety rolled down, and the F tight end is left open in the flat. If the corner triggers on the flat, the deep cross from the other side of the field will attack the vacated space.

Why it Didn't Work: The fake crossing route shown in the 6th diagram was called in week 16. This concept took a little too long to develop so Rodgers hits the check down for a positive gain.

Low Red Zone Specials

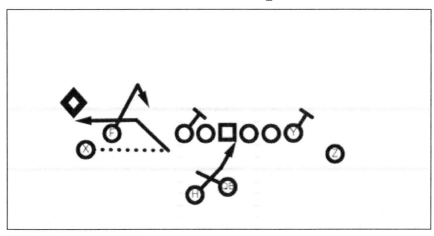

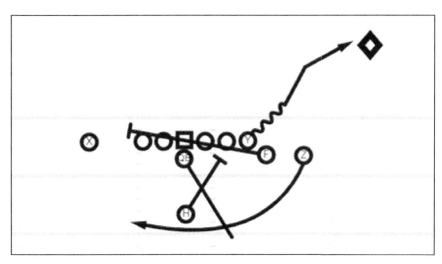

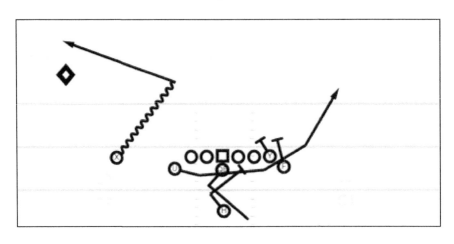

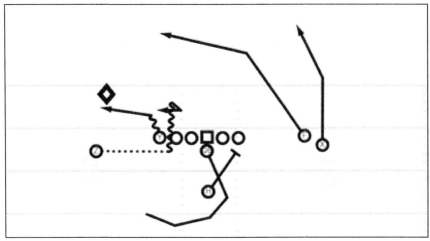

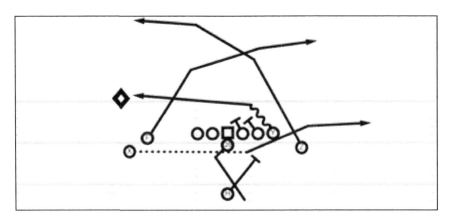

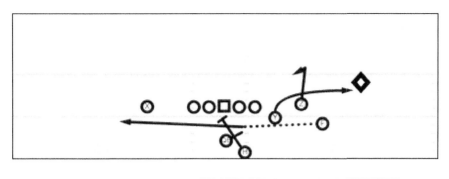

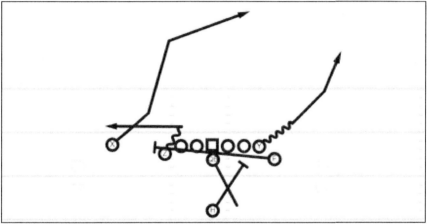

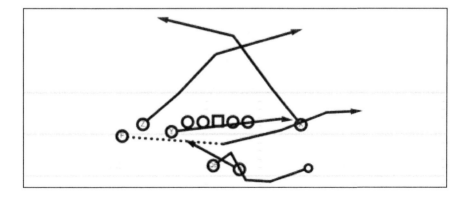

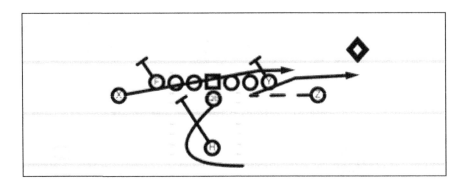

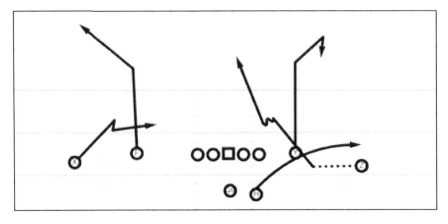

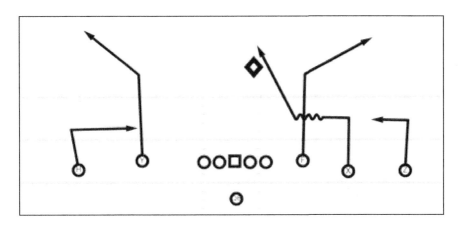

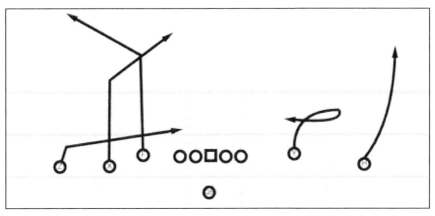

Average Yards per Play	2.9

1st Down		3rd/4th Down (includes RZ)	
Called	Average	Called	Success Rate
7	2.6	5	60%
2nd Down 6-1		**2nd Down 7+**	
Called	Average	Called	Average
3	3.3	1	8.0
Red Zone 10-0		**Red Zone 10-20**	
Called	Touchdown %	Called	Touchdown %
16	69%	0	0%

Cover 1		Cover 2		Cover 0	
Called	Average	Called	Average	Called	Average
7	4.4	0	0	5	0.8
Cover 3		**Cover 4**		**Cover 42**	
Called	Average	Called	Average	Called	Average
0	0.0	3	2.0	0	0
Cover 5		**Drop 8**		**5 Man Pressure**	
Called	Average	Called	Average	Called	Average
0	0	0	0	2	2.5

Week	Quarter	Time	Down	ToGo	Location	Yards
Week 7 vs HOU	1	9:26	3	3	HTX 3	3
Week 7 vs HOU	2	13:38	2	3	HTX 3	3
Week 8 vs MIN	2	6:57	1	1	MIN 1	1
Week 9 vs SF	2	7:05	1	1	SFO 1	1
Week 10 vs JAX	4	9:11	1	6	JAX 6	6
Week 12 vs CHI	2	15:00	1	5	CHI 5	5
Week 14 vs DET	3	7:13	1	10	DET 10	0
Week 14 vs DET	4	12:07	1	4	DET 4	4
Week 15 vs CAR	1	10:46	2	4	CAR 8	7
Week 15 vs CAR	1	9:58	1	1	CAR 1	1
Week 15 vs CAR	2	14:15	3	6	CAR 6	6
Week 16 vs TEN	3	10:33	2	8	OTI 8	8
DIV vs LAR	2	11:40	3	1	RAM 1	1
NFCCG vs TB	2	5:07	3	6	TAM 6	0
NFCCG vs TB	3	0:31	2	2	TAM 2	0
NFCCG vs TB	4	2:15	3	8	TAM 8	0

Having creative concepts in the low red zone gives your offense a chance when the defense can out-man you at the point of attack in the run game. Sometimes if you are not getting a good push with your base run schemes or your goal line runs, its good to have a few special plays in the bag.

The 2nd diagram shows the week 9 touchdown. Against man coverage, the in-line tight end will typically bluff the man that is guarding him. The orbit and slice action really draws attention to the other side of the field as well.

The 3rd diagram shows a long-developing play action concept used in week 10. The idea is to entice the corner to trigger the run fake, like he is being unblocked like he is so often against this offensive system.

The 4th diagram shows the week 12 touchdown to the tight end on the delay route. This concept could also fall into the Keeper Delay/Add section. The motion and run action entices the unblocked corner to trigger. The motion and run fake also keeps the strong safety off the tight end as he has to take on a block and fit his gap.

The 8th diagram shows a double slide concept used for a touchdown in week 7.

Why it Worked: The double cross variation shown in the fifth diagram scored vs Chicago in week 17.

Why it Didn't Work: The 9th diagram shows a fake jet misdirection concept used in the NFCCG. The Bucs communicated well and had two DB's to handle the motion and quick flat routes.

Slip Screens

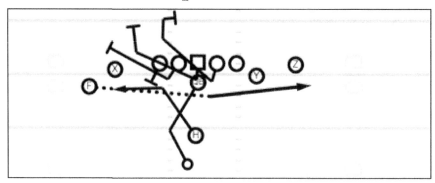

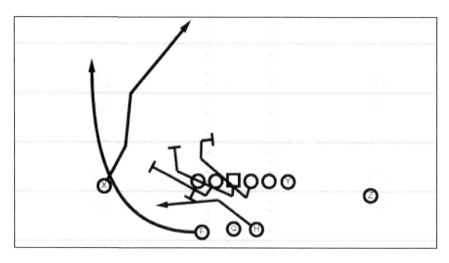

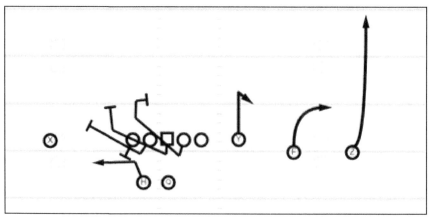

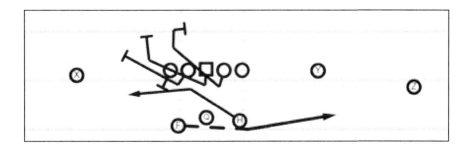

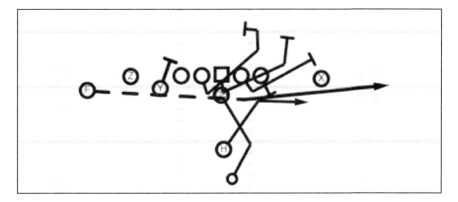

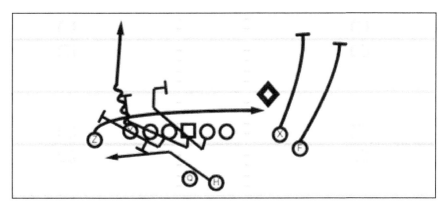

Average Yards per Play	7.6

1st Down		3rd/4th Down (includes RZ)	
Called	Average	Called	Success Rate
7	7.9	3	0%
2nd Down 6-1		**2nd Down 7+**	
Called	Average	Called	Average
2	5.5	6	6.3
Red Zone 10-0		**Red Zone 10-20**	
Called	Touchdown %	Called	Touchdown %
0	0%	0	0%

Bear		Over		6-Man	
Called	Average	Called	Average	Called	Average
1	9.0	9	7.4	0	0.0
Under (4 Man)		**Mug**		**Under Sam Up**	
Called	Average	Called	Average	Called	Average
3	2.7	0	0.0	0	0.0
Wide		**Odd**		**Diamond**	
Called	Average	Called	Average	Called	Average
5	10.4	1	13.0	0	0.0

Cover 1		Cover 2		Cover 0	
Called	Average	Called	Average	Called	Average
7	7.3	2	4.5	0	0
Cover 3		**Cover 4**		**Cover 42**	
Called	Average	Called	Average	Called	Average
5	7.8	3	8.0	0	0
Cover 5		**Drop 8**		**5 Man Pressure**	
Called	Average	Called	Average	Called	Average
0	0	1	10.0	0	0

Week	Quarter	Time	Down	ToGo	Location	Yards
Week 3 vs NO	1	4:27	1	10	GNB 35	5
Week 3 vs NO	4	9:33	2	7	NOR 32	0
Week 4 vs ATL	1	9:05	1	10	GNB 34	9
Week 4 vs ATL	2	1:07	3	15	ATL 41	13
Week 4 vs ATL	4	8:09	1	10	ATL 28	-3
Week 6 vs TB	3	2:09	2	13	GNB 22	-1
Week 7 vs HOU	2	0:49	1	10	HTX 23	15
Week 8 vs MIN	4	4:55	1	10	GNB 38	5
Week 9 vs SF	1	13:11	2	4	GNB 47	15
Week 9 vs SF	2	10:24	2	4	SFO 21	-4
Week 9 vs SF	3	5:27	1	10	SFO 47	24
Week 10 vs JAX	1	8:01	3	17	GNB 48	10
Week 10 vs JAX	2	11:52	2	13	GNB 24	11
Week 10 vs JAX	4	12:04	2	9	GNB 26	0
Week 13 vs PHI	1	6:26	3	23	GNB 12	9
Week 13 vs PHI	2	2:27	2	10	PHI 45	14
Week 15 vs CAR	2	2:00	1	10	CAR 41	0
Week 16 vs TEN	1	5:09	2	9	GNB 21	14

Slip Screens can be found in most NFL offenses. They are a common play call to discourage blitzes and aggressive up-field pass rushes.

The front side guard will be the first out on the screen (typically). He will kick out the force player. The center is typically the 2nd guy out, and he will lead up through the alley. The back side guard is typically the "clean up" guy to take any defensive lineman that are trying to chase the play from behind.

The Packers would often PSO (Pass-Screen Option) the slip screen with the Stick concept. The 3rd diagram shows this concept.

The 6th diagram shows the big play in week 13. Another PSO, this time with the drive concept. Against man coverage, the tight end sets a "pick" for the Z receiver coming under.

Why it Worked: The 24 yard gain in week 9 came against a blitz to the same side as the screen. The running back bluffs the blitzer and Rodgers times it up perfectly.

Why it Didn't Work: In week 15, the Panthers bring edge pressure to the side of the screen. The weak linebacker coming off the edge sniffs the play out forcing Rodgers to throw it away.

Reverses

Week	Quarter	Time	Down	ToGo	Location	Yards
Week 1 vs MN	1	1:14	1	10	MIN 44	19
Week 3 vs NO	1	2:05	1	10	NOR 31	-2
Week 7 vs HOU	4	6:22	2	6	HTX 42	9
Week 8 vs MIN	2	8:56	2	10	MIN 17	4

ABOUT THE AUTHOR

Bobby currently coaches at Maine East High School, in Park Ridge Illinois. You can find more of his work at:

www.theofficialpetersreport.blogspot.com

Email: bpeters1212@gmail.com

Other Books on Amazon

The 2017 New England Patriots Pass Game Manual

The 2019 San Francisco 49ers Complete Offensive Manual

The 2019 Tampa Bay Buccaneers Pass Game Index

The 2018 Chicago Bears Complete Offensive Manual

The 2017 Los Angeles Rams Third Down Manual

The 2017 Philadelphia Eagles Third Down Manual

The Melting Pot: How to Acclimate Old NFL Concepts into Your High School or College Offense

Quarterback Development: How Four NFL Teams Coached Their Quarterback to Have A Successful 2016 Season

The Complete Third Down Manual: The 2016 New Orleans Saints